Yes, please. Thanks!

Penny Palmano

Illustrations: Katherine Pershall

Panic Publishing (UK)

ACKNOWLEDGMENTS
Many thanks to Hazel Robinson for her editorial services and advice, David Spear and Roger on the editorial team. Katherine, my daughter, for the cartoons. Vicki Scarborough from Acorn Nursery and Sue Furby from the Hazelwood Infant School for their input. Jacqui McCarthy for her PR skills. Nicky Pensotti, Kjeld and James Taylor for their patience. Alan for the cover and Brian Lennon for his diagrams and finally, Keith Young, headmaster of Westbrook Hay School, for his foreword and wise words.

British Library Cataloguing in Publication Data Palmano, Penny

ISBN 0-9520396-1-3

First published in Great Britain in 2004 by:
Panic Publishing (UK)
Thornbie House
Donkey Lane
Bourne End
Buckinghamshire
SL8 5RR
Tel: 01628 810 874
Fax: 01628 522 519
e-mail: panic@palmano.com
www.panicpublishing.co.uk

Editor: Hazel Robinson

Editorial Team: David Spear, Keith Young

Illustrations: Katherine Pershall

Printed by: Unwin Brothers Ltd. The Gresham Press, Old Woking, Surrey GU22 9LH.

Typeset by: Pinewood Media Ltd, High Wycombe, Buckinghamshire. HP12 3QH.

Cover and Design: Alan Reinl Ltd, 54 Old Street, London EC1

Title: Hub Promotions Ltd, 1st Floor, Middlesex House, 34-42 Cleveland Street, London W1T 4JE

Cover and Back Photographs: Sonya Winner at Modern Photography, www.modernphotography.net

Cover models: Paris Palmano, Freya Wentworth-Stanley, Belle Palmano

Website design: Ryan Mullins, Latata Ltd, www.latata.co.uk

Book distribution: Gazelle Book Services Ltd, White Cross Mills, High Town, Lancaster, LA1 4XS

Printed May 2004
First Reprint June 2004

i

For
my mother
who has always been a wonderful example

Contents

FOREWORD

When Penny told me of her intention to write a book on children's manners and respect, I immediately thought of her son's progress through my school. If anyone better typified what can be done with good manners and respect then I haven't had the pleasure of seeing them yet. So, a little like a top chef giving advice on recipes, there is the instinctive confidence in the fact that Penny knows what she is talking about (and she is also a great cook!). The premise of this book is the desire to show parents what can be achieved, if they are willing to invest a little time and a great deal of consistency in the upbringing of their children. Parenting skills have noticeably declined over the years, as is evident in some of the behaviour witnessed in school, where seemingly the only guidance children have comes from the environment that surrounds them for their time at school. While the much more relaxed relationships between adults and children is to be commended and welcomed, the lack in many young children of the basic tenets of good manners and respect is highly regrettable. They are surrounded by poor examples in the society in which they live. Much of the television they watch or the music they listen to and even their heroes and idols offers them scant guidance as to how best to behave and the void that has opened between what used to be taken for granted and what is now accepted is a worrying trend.

The beauty of this book is there is something for everyone and there should be no fixed point at which people reading it need to start. Much will come down to personal preference and the kind of children that you want to raise. However, if good manners and respect still means something to you, the sagacity of the following chapters will provide you with an invaluable resource as you embark on the most difficult and rewarding journey that any adult can take – namely the fostering of a partnership with your offspring that is abiding and enriching and equips them with life skills that will shape and mark them as worthy individuals.

Keith Young, Headmaster, Westbrook Hay School, Hemel Hempstead, Herts.

INTRODUCTION

Firstly, I must point out that I am not a child 'expert', I am simply a mother who decided that if I was going to have children, they were going to be well-behaved, polite children that I could be proud of.

My experience with other children came from working as a nanny, teaching children to ski and then looking after children while their parents skied at a chalet business I ran with my first husband for six years. The one thing I learnt from all the different children I looked after, including my own, is all children respond to love, laughter, kind, calm and firm guidance.

Call me old fashioned but I like children to be well-mannered, have good table manners and be polite and respectful. I wanted to have children that I could take out in the knowledge that if we went to a restaurant their behaviour would not give me severe indigestion and apoplexy, even if the food and service did.

My children, like so many these days, did not have the benefit of the traditional Mum and Dad situation as I separated from their father when they were small. So from a young age they had to experience living with their single working mother, moving away from family and friends, changing schools, then along came a new step-father, step-sister, new family, new home, new school, new life. Changes and new challenges just makes a parent's job tougher, but does not excuse us from teaching manners, politeness and social skills to our children.

Newspapers, teachers, nannies and even grandparents (when they're not too busy spending our inheritance) all bemoan the fact that children seem now to be in control of their parents and to be honest in many cases they are right. But strangely enough little guidance seems to be forthcoming to these parents (who we imagine would prefer it otherwise).

There's been so many conflicting ideas of parenting over the past 40 years that mothers don't know whether to congratulate their child on being expressive when they pour tomato sauce into their favourite (saved up for years) Gucci shoes or take them for psychological counselling. (Psychological counselling? Surely I mean *adoption!*)

The word "No" appears to be politically incorrect and is almost obsolete in parenting today. Everything must be discussed. *Discuss, with a toddler!?* Gentle discipline and explanation, yes. *But discuss?*

Has the world gone mad?

I'm not Mother Earth. In fact, when I found out I was pregnant I asked my GP if I could have a general anaesthetic for the birth and suggested *being kept under for the next eighteen years.* Thankfully he refused because I would have missed out on eighteen wonderful years and, yes, obviously a few nightmares along the way.

Our children are now 15, 16 and 18 and I can honestly say that they have always been a joy to have around, loving, funny, polite, very well-mannered, respectful and popular with their own and our friends. They help around the house (when asked, not usually voluntarily), though I must mention the time they cleared-up after our Christmas party unpromted (after their parents and 50 plus friends had called it a night). *What angels.* My sister-in-law says they are the bench mark that all children should be judged by. High praise indeed. Perfect? Of course not, they don't keep their rooms tidy and they wouldn't know how to pick up a wet towel off their bathroom floor if their life depended on it. But in the big picture does it matter?

Our responsibility as parents is to teach our children discipline, manners, respect and the social skills so they will develop into well-adjusted happy young adults. It's no surprise that children who are taught these qualities are higher achievers at school, make friends more easily and are more popular with their teachers and other adults.

There are no set rules for bringing up children, how can there be when they are all individual? Bringing up families can and should be fun and I hope this advice will help you enjoy your children to the full. It's hard to enjoy your children when you're constantly berating and arguing with them, but it needn't be that way.

Bringing up children is 90% common sense and 10% struggling through, although there are many, many times when these percentages seem to completely swap places! So, I hope this book helps you get started or puts you back on the right track. It will not answer every question or solve every problem but it will help you end up with happy, confident and trustworthy children you can justifiably be really proud of and make your life as a parent much easier and less stressful.

Good luck. It's worth it!

THE BUCK STOPS HERE

Everything we buy these days comes with hard and fast care instructions. Whether it's a pair of knickers or a frying pan we are told exactly how to look after them.

But a child doesn't come with instructions. We simply leave home one day and return with a small human life which is totally dependent on us for love, food, comfort, education, clothing, housing and for bringing him or her up to be a well-balanced, well-behaved, confident child that can go out into the world as a well adjusted young adult. *WHAT!? The responsibility of it all is enough to make any parent break out in a sweat and lay down in a darkened room with a large, nerve-calming drink.*

So is it a lottery and simply good luck if we have well-behaved children that are a delight to be around or incredible bad luck that we end up with uncontrollable, rude, disrespectful little 'horrors' that are a constant nightmare and embarrassment to us?

Let's face it, how many times have we thought or said about someone else's children:

"Why on earth does she let *those* children do that?"
"Just as long as they don't bring those *ghastly* children"
"Did you see the way that child was eating?"

Imagine if these comments were directed at your own children? Now don't panic even if you suspect they already have been and don't criticise or label yourself a bad parent and accept things the way they are, just address the problem. Get back in control.

The good news is that all children can be brought up to be well-behaved, well-mannered, polite and respectful, regardless of their personality or character. Obviously all children are different and a very strong-willed child may need a stronger sense of his boundaries than a calmer, quieter child but both can be equally well-behaved and a credit to their parents.

But how?
Teaching manners and respect starts almost from day one, the way we are with our children from very early days will start to form and mould the way they

are going to behave. So basically, it's easier if we don't let them get into bad habits and then try and correct them. It is so much easier, for everyone concerned, if they learn everything the right way from the beginning, not dissimilar to puppy training.

For example, if we take a puppy to training classes from as early as possible, he will learn to walk correctly on a lead, sit and stay when told. But if we don't train it from an early age, by the time we realise our dog is uncontrollable and we decide to start teaching him, our problems are ten fold. That old saying, 'One word from me, and he does as he likes,' can equally be said about some children.

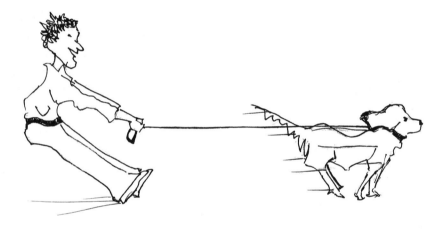

The sooner you start the easier it is !

Manners and respect in the 21st Century – why we still need them

Manners, respect and simple courtesies should be second nature to everyone. They show a consideration for our fellow man and are a condition of a civilised society. The acid test to our children's behaviour is how others perceive it. Their social education is as important as their academic one. So come on, put in that time and effort, after all don't they deserve the best?

HOW THE WRONG FOODS CAN AFFECT CHILDREN'S BEHAVIOUR, HEALTH AND IQ!

There's no point trying to teach your children how to behave when the food and drink they are consuming is working against you both. It's like wanting a good night's sleep but drinking a gallon of Turkish coffee an hour before bedtime! It simply isn't going to happen.

The scary facts

Most children eat far too many fast food products, pre-prepared meals, processed foods, fizzy drinks, snacks, sweets, biscuits, cakes, etc and almost all these products may contain some type of food colouring, preservative salt and sugar. The additives are a kind of 'food cosmetic make-over', disguising poor nutritional food with colour and artificial flavour to make it more attractive to children.

But the increased consumption of these foods and the decline in the foods which are good for children, such as fresh vegetables, fruit, fish, meat and cheese, has sadly begun to take its toll. **Hyperactivity, moodiness, obesity, long-term health problems and poor intellectual performance can all be connected to a poor diet.**

Behaviour and food

For years and years parents have voiced their concern about the possible link between food colourings, preservatives and behavioural changes in their children, but the food manufacturers and government were constantly dismissive claiming their theories lacked scientific evidence.

However, results from the first UK government sponsored analysis have shown that in a study children who are given colourings and preservatives in a fruit juice, were reported by their parents of **'fiddling with objects'**, **'disturbing others'**, **'difficulty settling down to sleep'**, **'difficulty concentrating'** and **'temper tantrums'**.

The researchers further claimed that if the problem additives and preservatives were removed from children's diets, hyperactivity would be reduced from 1 in 6 children to 1 in 17.

Health and food
In this health conscious, diet addicted era in which we now live, during the past ten years there has been a 70% increase in obesity among three and four year olds. *Obesity in three to four years olds!!!!???* If this doesn't ring alarm bells what will? When many mothers are on some kind of diet why are we letting our children become obese under our very noses?

If that isn't scary enough it is now recognised that **obesity leads to increased risks of heart disease and diabetes.**

The cause is quite simply a poor diet and lack of exercise.

Poor diet
Although children enjoy eating crisps, sweets, snacks and processed foods and however quick and convenient they may be for the parent, these foods are the culprits.

Too much salt
Too much salt will withdraw calcium from the body which children urgently need to develop strong bones, teeth and nails. It will also **increase the risk of osteoporosis, asthma, strokes, heart attacks, water retention and raised blood pressure in later life.**

Too much Sugar
For years we have known that sugar has disastrous effects on children's teeth and contributes towards obesity. But it is also a stimulant which affects children's blood sugar levels producing short **bursts of energy or hyperactivity** immediately after an intake, followed by an immediate low, which can manifest itself in **moodiness** or **difficult behaviour** and a craving for more sugar.

The brain chemicals which affect people's moods including depression are called serotonin and beta endorphins. Doctors now believe that there is a direct link between glucose (what pure white sugar breaks down into in our bodies) and these chemicals.

An excess of white sugar can change the normal biochemical 'pathways' of both, **resulting in moody, unmanageable and disruptive children** who make everyone's life a misery, including their own. Products made mainly from pure white flour will also convert into pure sugar in the body with the same effect.

A can of a popular well-known fizzy drink contains both sugar and caffeine, combining *two* stimulants. If children drink a **can at lunchtime the caffeine will still be in their system by the evening** and we know what that means, T-R-O-U-B-L-E. These poor children **will not be able to sit still** at school or around the dinner table and will find it **difficult to fall asleep**. Be on the safe side and avoid all sugary foods at supper-time, offer fruit as an alternative dessert or snack.

To reduce children's intake of sugar take the sugar bowl off the table and be in charge of the amount they can have. Gradually reducing the sugar on their cereals and in their diet will go unnoticed but will make a significant difference to their overall consumption.

Schools that have removed vending machines selling sugar laden snacks and drinks and replaced them with fresh fruit and water or fruit juice have reported that attention rates have improved and that problem children are much calmer as a result.

Give your children fresh or dried fruit, water and juices (check the sugar content) as snacks and leave the sweet snacks and drinks for the odd occasion or use them on a reward basis occasionally. As an alternative to canned fizzy drinks dilute fruit concentrates with a fizzy mineral water. Your children's tastes will adapt to their healthy diet and although they will still enjoy sweet products they will find many unnaturally sweet.

Fats

Much has been written about fats in the body. It is now widely recognised that the body does need fat and that there are both good and bad fats.

Good fats

The brain is composed of 60% fat and needs an abundance of fatty acids from our diet to function effectively. Essential fatty acids are the good fats. They are found in oily fish such as mackerel, tuna, herring, sardines and salmon and nuts, seeds and cold-pressed oils. These fatty acids are essential for the

5

normal development of the brain, eyes and nervous system. New research from Oxford University has indicated that many children suffering from dyslexia, dyspraxia and ADHD (attention deficit hyperactive disorder) which **affect children's ability to listen, think, speak, sit still and write** are suffering from a dietary deficiency of fatty acids.

Bad fats
However, most processed foods, fried foods and convenience foods contain trans fats. Trans fats are formed by hydrogenating oils in order to improve their shelf-life and flavour. Trans fats alter the brain chemistry and block the production of the essential fatty acids

Always read the label

Until the food industry starts to reduce the amount of salt, sugar, preservatives and additives in their products always read the label.

Even some foods that proudly claim on their labels, 'NO artificial sweeteners' and 'NO preservatives' may still have added colourings.

Steer well clear of:
Colours: Tartrazine E102, Sunset Yellow E110, Carmoisine E122, Ponceau 4R E124
Preservatives: Sodium Benzoate E211
Saturated fats and anything 'Hydrogenated'

"But my children love fizzy drinks and snacks"

There is nothing wrong with the occasional packet of crisps or a fizzy drink, but they should not be part of the daily diet.
If we keep sugar-laden drinks, high fat snacks and sweets in the house, the temptation for our children to ask/moan/beg for them is quite natural. So to avoid having any confrontation, only buy them for when you want them, perhaps for a weekend.
Quite simply, if these products are not in the house, there is no issue, and everyone is much healthier and happier all round.

Getting off to a good start – breakfast

The British Nutrition Foundation urge all parents to ensure that their children eat breakfast to improve their performance at school. Researchers have reported that foods with a low glycemic index (GI) are far better for your children than foods with a high glycemic index. But, as we all have busy lives to lead, I'll cut to the chase, wholegrain breads, porridge, muesli and high–fibre cereals are good (low GI). Cereals such as cornflakes or chocolate flavoured cereals and white bread are not (high GI).

Children who eat a low GI breakfast will be less hungry at lunchtime and less likely to want to snack between meals.

Children who eat a high GI breakfast will have an initial energy boost then feel sluggish. They will be hungrier by lunchtime and are far more likely to snack.

Research on children aged 9 – 16 given sugar laden snacks for breakfast (simple carbohydrates) reacted and gave levels of performance of 70 year-olds!

Healthy breakfasts may include a combination of the following, smoothies, (yogurt and fruit shakes) fresh milk shakes with fruit, wholegrain toast with peanut butter or banana, a boiled egg, fresh fruit, high-fibre cereal and fruit juice, milk or water to drink.

Exercise

Try and get your children to exercise as often as possible.
By restricting your children's TV and computer time it should be easier to get them outside whether it's for a game of Frisbee in the park or walking to the shops. If they enjoy sport encourage them to join a local club.

Invest in a battery operated dance mat or one which plugs into the Playstation, children will dance away for hours following the 'right steps'.

The school run

So many children are chauffeured everywhere these days that the opportunity to walk has been severely curtailed. Sadly, as a result of today's society, parents are also concerned about the risk their children may be exposed to by walking in public. One solution is to drive part of the way to school and to walk the remainder with your child.

Teenagers eating habits

If children grow up aware that their mothers have been perpetually trying new diets, weighing themselves and commenting on their weight, they may well grow up with the same anxieties which can lead to eating disorders.

Growing teenagers are permanently hungry and are happy to continually graze on snacks throughout the day (the expression 'eating me out of house and home' springs to mind), so rather than fill the cupboards with sugar laden, high fat snacks make sure that there are plenty of healthy snacks in the house, fresh fruit, dried fruit, nuts, seeds, plain biscuits, brown wholegrain bread and fillings for sandwiches and toasties. If you buy crisps, choose the low-fat variety.

Home-cooking and eating as a family around the table is the easiest way to make sure the family have a good nutritional evening meal and a way of seeing exactly what your teenager is eating.

Comfort foods

We've all been there, feeling low and depressed. And the first thing we do is hit the biscuit tin then feel more depressed that we ate most of the contents. As we would much prefer our children never turn to food for comfort, try to avoid giving them treat foods as a consolation when they are growing up. Try and start a new regime of going for a walk or some other type of exercise if you are feeling low. The fresh air and exercise will immediately start to make you feel better.

Respecting other children's dietary needs

Always respect the dietary needs of children visiting your home. Their parents will tell you what they must avoid and to make life easier on everyone simply do not have that product available to your own children on that particular day. I only mention this because I knew of a situation where a mother had a child to play with her children who was hypersensitive to sugar and she gave him a biscuit as a 'treat'. The child who was too young to realise any different, ate it, and was as high as a kite for about four days.

WHAT CHILDREN REALLY NEED

Forget the DVD's, T.V.'s, Playstations, designer trainers and designer clothes (except obviously, for us). What children really need, (as opposed to think they need) is a combination of love, discipline, attention, communication, respect, example, routine, consistency and continuity, and wouldn't that be simple if we could just go and buy it. But nobody said bringing up children was going to be simple. As every child is different only you will work out how much of all these vital components your particular child needs to find the right combination.

LOVE

How to show love

Our children need to feel and know that they are loved, that unconditional love that only we, their parents can give them which is not tied to the way they behave or perform and cannot be withdrawn as a means of manipulation. Love needs to be shown in different ways, by physical affection, by showing respect and acceptance and by the way we care and nurture our children.

From day one, babies physically and mentally need bodily contact to bond to their parents. And it's not just as babies they need to be cuddled, but all through their developing years to adulthood. Even adults enjoy a hug with their parents. Children need the reassurance that physical contact in the form of kisses and cuddles, a stroke of the cheek, or an arm around a shoulder can provide. We can reinforce how we feel by actually telling them that they are loved.

Far too many parents neglect, unintentionally, to demonstrate enough physical contact to their children as they grow up. And whilst a fourteen year old may dislike showing any physical emotion towards their parents in front of their friends, they will be just as happy to have a hug with their mother or father when they get home.

Parents who had a loving childhood may find it easier to show love than parents who were deprived of physical love as children, so some parents have to make more effort to be physical, but it is absolutely essential that children never have to question their parents' love for them.

Young children enjoy seeing their parents showing affection to each other, it's

10

just as they get older they get horribly embarrassed.

Love must also be shown by guiding and educating your children so that they can function happily in their environment. It must never be confused with putting your hand in your pocket.

There are two ways of showing love, one is the cuddly love of hugs and kisses and the other is the equally important one of teaching your child how to behave.

Little things mean a lot

Apart from the usual ways in which we can show our love for our children, they also appreciate little kind, thoughtful gestures, just as we like our partners to do for us. For instance, if they have a test at school, let them know you are thinking of them by sending a good luck text with an encouraging message, 'Thinking of you. Go show 'em. You can do it, Luv u, Mum'. If you know that they're a bit low because they didn't make the football team or get the part in the school play they wanted, surprise them with their favourite treat to help cheer them up. Or once they've left for school you discover they have left an important piece of school-work at home, make the effort to take it to the school. Don't just think, "Oh they're always forgetting things, this'll teach them," or turn up at the school and give your child a lecture on getting organised before you hand the work over. Be loving, be kind. They will learn to be more organised. When you see the look of relief on their faces simply say with a smile, "It's a good job I love you so much".

Sometimes just give your child a big hug and tell them you just couldn't resist doing it because they are so gorgeous. Wouldn't we all love it if our partners (still/ever) did that? But perhaps if we did it to them, they might!

DISCIPLINE

It's our responsibility

The very word discipline disappeared almost completely from parenting for many years because we all grew up to associate discipline with harsh punishment, but what it really means is teaching our children how to behave so they can eventually control their own behaviour. In fact the word discipline is derived from the Latin word *disciplina* meaning instruction and not as you may have thought, "A darn good spanking."

Don't worry they will love you any less because you have to be occasionally firm with them, they will in fact love you all the more when they realise they have grown into socially acceptable, functional adults.

How we start to impose discipline on our children

- Boundaries
- Change voice and body language
- Orders are not negotiable
- Continuity and consistency
- Make rules clear and simple
- Tell children what you expect of them
- Encourage and reward good behaviour
- Be firm about poor behaviour
- Teaching why "No" must always mean "No"
- Remain calm and in control

Boundaries

Boundaries are the sets of rules we set for our children's behaviour; a sort of framework of moral conduct within which they must learn to live. As long as children know exactly where these limits are they will be happy and content to operate within them. Naturally most children will try and stretch them occasionally to see exactly what they can get away with, but this is absolutely normal and they are quite expecting and relieved to be told when they have crossed the line. Let's face it we all try and push our luck sometimes.

Boundaries teach children what is acceptable behaviour and in doing so they develop the self-control and self-discipline necessary to remain within them.

Even children from as young as one will begin to respond to simple boundaries, as in the word 'No', when it is said in a firm voice distinguishable from your normal voice.

Inevitably, as children grow up, new boundaries will be introduced, but as long as they know what they are, they will flourish and develop within them and be reassured by them.

However, children who are not set boundaries often feel unloved and uncared for and are constantly floundering for some sort of guidelines, usually in the form of unacceptable behaviour, as if in a desperate plea for some sort of help and structure. Without boundaries children fail to develop self-control without which they will find it difficult to function properly within a normal society and can end up unhappy, lonely and dysfunctional adults.

Change voice and body language

From as young as a year old, your child can begin to learn the meaning of the word, "No". Adopt a low, firm tone and deliver a short sharp, "No", so that they can recognise disapproval immediately and do not smile. There's no point saying "No," in exactly the same sweet tone that you would say "Hello darling" with a beaming smile on your face. Equally don't say "No" in a firm voice and then immediately give your child hugs and cuddles as it is mixing messages. Even young children will come to recognise when parents are in "no mood for messing with" by their voice and body language.

If, for instance, your daughter is at the stage of moving around holding on to the furniture and she grabs an ornament you would rather she did not touch, you simply say, 'No', in a firm voice, remove the ornament from her and move her to a different part of the room. Give your daughter a toy or something else to distract her that she can look at and examine. Many children will immediately return to the ornament and look for your reaction. Make sure it is the same. As soon as your child starts showing an interest in something they can play with, praise them and make a fuss of them. At this age they very soon learn when Mummy approves or disapproves. Suddenly your daughter has learnt her first boundary. She knows that she cannot touch the ornament.

Orders are not negotiable

We have all witnessed a poor mother who asks her child to do something and is either ignored or rebuffed or argued with. Out of frustration the parent either shouts at the child to no avail or does the task herself.

"Please go and fetch the blue sweater off my bed," is a command. It is not negotiable, "*Would* you like to go and fetch my sweater off my bed?" is negotiable. If you ask your child to do something for you, insist that they do it. It is so important that children learn to respond to instructions. Giving and taking orders are all part of life's rules and children must not be allowed to imagine they are somehow immune to it. School, the workplace, even leisure activities will require orders to be acted upon, sometimes immediately.

To make it less stressful all round, (although this will not always be possible) try not to ask for something you want an immediate response to if your child is engrossed in an activity, a book, in the middle of a favourite TV programme time or doing their homework. If they are busy concentrating on something, they are more likely to show some resistance. In these circumstances ask them to carry out your request after they have finished the chapter, TV programme or their homework and make sure they have heard and understood.

Warning children in advance that they will have to do something will help prepare them mentally to do it, as in "Dinner will be ready in five minutes," then after that time, "Come and sit down, please."

Children disobeying orders can be life-threatening. For example, if a young boy has never been taught to obey his mother, one day he gets separated from her in a car park, then suddenly sees her. She shouts, "Stay there, don't move, there's a car coming," and the child doesn't, he is putting himself and possibly others at risk.

A good way to get children to obey first time requests is to ask them to do something quickly so that they can have a reward or get on with doing something far more fun. For instance, if a mother is returning home with her children, "Quickly, go and hang your coats up and then you can have a biscuit/start painting". Then when they return, "You've put your coats away already? That's fantastic, my goodness you're fast. Well done, here's your biscuit/right if you get the paints out, I'll get the paper." Suddenly children are in the mind-set to help. They soon learn that doing as asked brings praise and rewards.

Of course, there are going to be far many more times when you will simply ask them to do something without dangling the carrot and they must react as quickly. When you are teaching your young children to obey simple commands, explain what you would like them to do, keep it simple, ask if they understand then wait and watch to see them do it. If they ignore you, repeat it and mention that you would like it done now. If they don't move immediately take their hand and help them up with a, "Come along, mummy has asked you to pick up your socks and to give them to me. Now pick them up like a good boy". Once the command has been carried out, thank them. If they carried out the task with no fuss, thank and congratulate them at their speed and efficiency. If they refuse to pick the socks up, put your hand over theirs and help them to pick up the socks then give them to yourself. Thank them in a matter-of-fact voice.

Persistence is the name of the game, do not leave the room until they have done what they were asked to do, keep a firm voice, do not lose your temper. Never let your children get away with not doing something they have been asked to do. It can be a small battle of wills, but you are the parent, you must be in control. When children realise that you are not going to give in, they will. You may only have to sit out two or three incidents like these until your children act upon your requests. That Mum or Dad mean business is a valuable lesson for children to learn. There will be times when they dawdle and don't react immediately, but don't let them get into a habit of just not doing it.

> I was recently at a taxi rank at a train station and there was a mother and her son of about 6. She asked him to put his empty plastic water bottle in the bin and pointed out where it was (about 10 yards away). The first and second time she asked he ignored her, the third time she asked he put it on a window ledge, the fourth time he took it off the window ledge and played with it. This scenario continued for a total of about 10 minutes when finally, the mother picked up the bottle, which had now been abandoned on the floor, took her son by his arm and walked him to the bin and dumped it for him.

When the son disobeyed after the first request the mother should have taken him to the bin then and made him throw the bottle away, even if she had to put it in his hand at the final moment before it was dumped. She should have praised him for dumping it then immediately talked about something else. By allowing her son to disobey her request several times she inadvertently taught him that he has the option whether to do as he has been asked or not and if he decides not to his mother will do it anyway.

Continuity and consistency
Rules that you create must be upheld by you and your partner. If for instance, children have been told that something is off limits, it must always be off limits not just occasionally. Your partner must also know what is off limits and what action to take if they disobey.

Children learn by consistency, so your children must always be treated in the same way if they do something that displeases.

It's very easy when you are tired or depressed not to stick to the rules and your children will soon learn that you sometimes give in if they ignore them. Hard as it is sometimes when you are tired, always stand your ground over rules. In the long run it will make life so much easier.

Make rules clear and simple
Always be specific about what your children should or should not do. Telling children to "Behave nicely" or "Eat properly" can mean very little, but if you say, "Take your feet off the sofa" or "Use your spoon", you are making yourself very clear.

Tell them what you expect of them
Once your children have learned to obey simple commands, if you are going out whether it is to a restaurant, the cinema or to the shops, talk to them before you go and let them know exactly how you would like them to behave. Children are often better behaved if they are prepared and they know exactly what is expected of them.

Encourage and reward good behaviour
The most positive 'new' parenting skill to have emerged over the past twenty years is the encouragement and reward of good behaviour and paying less attention to poor. Children, as we have already said, love attention and the praise and positive attention they receive from behaving well will spur them on to behave in that way again. Promising a reward for good behaviour is likely to produce more satisfactory results than threatening to punish bad behaviour.

We now know that children who receive litlle attention from their parents, will behave badly just to receive attention, even if that attention is a reprimand. Paying little or no attention to attention-seeking behaviour is likely to stop it.

Being firm about poor behaviour

However, I am not of the school that believes in completely ignoring poor behaviour. Children must immediately be told that whatever they were doing is unacceptable otherwise how will they ever know? If it persists, there is no discussion but an immediate penalty should be enforced. Parents who allow their children to always give a reason for their bad behaviour are only encouraging them constantly to make excuses and not accept responsibility for their actions and are storing up problems for the future. Children must learn to accept the consequences of their actions otherwise they will never accept blame even when they clearly *are* to blame. The constant drone from teenagers of, "It's not my fault," will in a way be correct as they had never been taught to be responsible for their actions.

Teaching why the word 'No', MUST ALWAYS MEAN 'No

But it's not the child's fault, as the parents have unintentionally trained him that way.

It is surprising how many children are taught that 'No' means 'Maybe' and to some, 'No' eventually means, 'Yes'.

Parents eventually giving in to their children's continual requests for something may seem harmless, but it will be a complete pain in the backside when, ten years down the line, it becomes a perpetual droning every time they want something.

And this is how it happens. For example, a toddler wants another biscuit and the parent says, "No." The toddler will then go on and on that she wants another biscuit. The parent still says, "No." Bear in mind toddlers have little conception of time. So the child continues to whine about the biscuit. The parent often becomes fed up with the whining and to keep the peace gives in and gives the child another biscuit with some lame response, such as, "Now this really is your last one".

By this seemingly harmless action, the child has been taught that although, "No," was said several times, if she whines long enough she will eventually get what she wants. And let's face it, at the time it may seem so much easier to give in than to hold your ground, but be firm. And don't be fooled by the dramatics, a young child begging for another biscuit then crying for just one more will pull at the old heart strings. Stand your ground. You are doing your child a disservice if you give in.

In a situation like this, if you have said, "No," remove the biscuits or the wanted item out of sight, and divert the child's attention with a toy, a book, a drawing, anything. If you are in company, don't be embarrassed, simply explain, you'll get far more respect than if you're seen to be giving in.

Try & stay calm

If you start this at an early age, a child will have learnt that "No," means "No," by the time they are three or four, and life will be much easier. This is not to say they will never ask a second or third time for something, after all you want them to show a bit of spirit, but they will expect and accept a definitive, "No."

Try and remain calm and in control

"Easier said than done!" you're probably thinking, when the children have been arguing all day, refuse to leave the TV and won't do their homework or tidy their room. In a perfect world we would never lose our tempers and shout at our children but in a perfect world our children would never do anything to make us. However, in the real world they do and sometimes we do lose it.

In such cases when you suddenly snap and scream or shout at your children, if they are young, they may burst into tears as they have never seen their mother or father in this state and it frightens them. As soon as you compose yourself apologise to them and say that you're sorry you lost your temper. Some young children may need to be reassured that although you shouted you still love them. Don't go thinking you are a terrible parent or having a guilt trip because you screamed a short monologue at your children. Firstly you are not alone and secondly you are a parent not a saint!

However, even older children can be upset by seeing a parent suddenly losing it. Again apologise, but do not let your sudden lack of control become the substitute for their punishment. If during your rant you unrealistically said that they were not going to go out for a month and anything still remaining on their bedroom floor was going to be binned, when you have composed yourself, impose a sensible punishment. If your children are not used to seeing you lose control, they too will feel guilty that they pushed you that far, where in truth it was possibly a combination of things culminating in something they did being, 'the straw that broke the camel's back'. If this is the case explain it to them, as children get older they can start to understand the pressures adults are put under with work, relationships, money issues and children.

Making a habit of shouting at your children will just teach them that, if you can't control yourself, how should they and they will revert to shouting and screaming when they are angry. Shouting is very ineffective and they will cease listening to what you are saying. Some children actually quite enjoy seeing a parent losing their self-control and will wind them up accordingly. Don't fall into that trap.

It is far more effective to speak in a very firm, very controlled voice, as if to say, "I am in control and I intend remaining very much in control."

Dealing with unsociable behaviour
1 – 4 years old

What to expect
Toddlers are as much maligned as teenagers, they are labelled rebellious, defiant even impossible. And yes they can be all those things. In fact both these development stages are similar, children battling for independence. Our mission as parents from day one is to help, guide and educate them towards that independance.

However, a few valuable points to remember about toddlers are:

• They have a short attention span

- They do not have the ability to see the consequences of their actions
- They are curious about everything
- They are easily distracted

So that said firstly, never forget that you are an adult. You are a responsible adult who can have a mortgage, drive a car, reproduce and earn a living. Your children may not yet be two, they probably can't hold a pencil correctly, hold a conversation or control their bowels. So there's no reason they should get the better of you, is there? *Is there?*

At around two your toddlers will start to assert themselves as the battle for their ultimate goal, independence, begins, which will incorporate winning and losing a few battles along the way. This two year period is actually the time when they suss out what sort of parents you are and how much they will be able to get away with in the future. **Their respect in you starts here.** Crack it now and life ahead will be easier for all of you. Although your children won't recognise it, they will feel reassured and safe knowing that their parents are there constantly guiding, helping, correcting and leading them on their long road to independence.

Children need and sub-consciously want boundaries and they need to know what they are. Keep rules simple so that they can understand, such as they are not allowed to hit the cat, or bang their sit-on car into the cupboard. Once they know their boundaries they will try and cross them. Very often they will watch for your reaction as they do it, as if to say, "So what are you going to do about it?" Do something about it. Stop them immediately, in these examples, remove the cat or the car. They will be so much happier for it (so will the cat).

When toddlers start to disagree with you it's not because they're being disrespectful, they just have a different opinion. If you were to have a toddler that just sat quietly in the corner and obeyed your every command, *then* worry!

Tantrums (theirs not yours)

Anytime onwards from when your children are about eighteen months you can prepare yourself for the onslaught of the tantrum, the 'terrible twos' as they are sometimes known. Toddlers should come with one those warnings you see at theme parks for the scary rides, 'If you suffer from a nervous disposition, high-blood pressure or a weak heart .....' but they don't and at times although you may wish to throw your arms in the air and scream, don't. Stay calm, keep control, you're in for a rollercoaster ride and when it's all over, just like the scary ride, you'll think it wasn't that bad after all.

Although there will be times when you wonder why you never noticed someone replace your beautiful baby with the spawn of Satan, just remember that children do not have tantrums to anger you. They have them because they are frustrated or angry and they simply don't know how to express themselves differently. All this said, **never, ever give in to a tantrum** otherwise they will still be throwing them when they are nineteen.

Tantrums are like one-man shows, they need an audience to survive and thrive. Remove the audience and the performance will quickly end.

Often there is some incident or response to an incident which 'lights the blue touch paper', and they're off, stamping feet, crying, lying on the floor and kicking, all terribly dramatic. If you are at home and they are not in danger of hurting themselves simply leave them where they are or put them into their bedroom, on a chair or the floor or the bed and leave. Do not close the door. Don't raise your voice, get angry or be rough.

Calmly tell them that when they stop crying and behaving in that way, they can come and see you. Then get out of sight, and stay out of sight until the child calms down. With no audience, they will soon stop. When they are calm they will either come to you or you go to them and explain how they should have expressed themselves. Then do not mention the incident again. It's history. Simply move on and suggest something to do, but never give a sweet or biscuit immediately after a tantrum as this may be seen by the child as a reward. *And that's the last thing we want.*

If your child is flailing around and you are worried that he might harm himself just hold him gently until he settles.

If the incident has been sparked by a sweet, or a sibling's toy, or a piece of clothing, remove it out of sight for the remainder of the day if possible. By the next day it will be forgotten.

And if they start to throw a tantrum in the supermarket immediately take them outside or back to the car and let them cool-off, then begin again. Under no circumstances decide to leave the food shopping for another day. When your children have settled down explain what you are going to do i.e. the shopping and would they help, if they do help they can have a reward of a sweet or comic afterwards.

Never give in when you are in public because of the fuss they are making. There are loads of parents who are going to recognise what's happening, we've all had children throwing screaming tantrums in public and we will all silently pat you on the back for seeing you do the right thing.

If your child is creating in his pushchair in the supermarket or shop and someone thinks it would be kind to offer the child a sweet, immediately thank them but take it and say that they can have it later.

The silent tantrum

The silent tantrum is where they lie on the floor face down and refuse to get up or move. This type of tantrum for some unknown reason does not seem to happen much at home. The little darlings seem to like to keep this gem for public outings, such as supermarkets and shops.

The best way to deal with this show of wills, is to ask them to get up, to which they will probably not reply, then calmly say that you are going home, and if they would like to come would they please come now. This will either be met with a stony silence or a, "No". If they happen to be lying in the middle of an aisle or in an inconvenient place (they're all inconvenient, you shout) simply say, "I'll just move you to one side (and do), because you are in everyone's way, now I'm off home, Goodbye." Move a few yards away, not letting them out of your sight, but slightly hidden so when they look up for you in about thirty seconds, they will not immediately see you. They will then probably get up and you can go and retrieve them and leave together.

You will soon get to know the warning signs of an impending tantrum, so far as possible try to avoid them.

How to try and avoid tantrums

- Try not to let your toddler get over tired. Stick to regular nap and sleep times.
- Keep to a daily routine as far as possible.
- Keep them regularly fed and watered especially before going out somewhere and take a healthy snack with you.
- Cancel going out if you feel your toddler is sickening for something or unwell.
- Avoid saying the word "No" to their every request, say "Perhaps", or "Maybe later," or "That sounds like a good idea." Of course, you must still use the word "No" for discipline.

Avoid arguing

The stand-up battle of wills as in, "You will…," "No, I won't," is only training your child to argue and to be avoided at all costs. So where possible find an alternative to the confrontation, it will be far less stressful for everyone concerned. If you would like your toddler to do something that you know he will not want to do, try not to ask directly. For instance, rather than say "Please undress for bed now", which for a toddler is just the perfect excuse to say, "No." Try a bit of reverse psychology as in, "I bet you can't get undressed in the time it takes me to run to the kitchen and fetch your drink, ready, steady go", which is far more likely to have them undressing as quickly as possible. And by the way, let them win. Tell them you can't believe how fast they were and the next time you'll have to run faster.

Responsibility

From the age of about two children like to start to feel responsible and as they are battling for their independence it's a good idea to give them some. You want to let your children think they are sometimes getting their way although they will be doing exactly what you want (just like husbands really!).

For example, getting dressed can often cause problems with young children so put out two outfits and ask them to choose which one they would like to wear. In their minds they have got their own way but then so have you. Everyone is happy. Ask them to try and get in the car seat themselves and do up their harness. Would they prefer to help Mummy make the beds first or dust the sitting room? Only ever give them a choice of two things.

Pushchairs are often a cause for a battle. If they don't want to get in, then if possible, let them push it, put reins or a child lead either on them or on the pushchair so you are still in some control.

Distraction
Toddlers have a very short concentration span and are easily diverted so use this to your advantage. On the verge of a strop (the toddlers not yours) or just starting to do something you rather they didn't, distract them. "Did you see that bird out the window, quick let's see if it's still there?" "Quick, come and see the spider running under the bed." OK there was no bird or spider but they don't know that and while they're looking for them they have completely forgotten what they were about to do. Use your imagination. Never forget you're an adult and they are not yet four.

How to avoid going mad
- Toddlerproof your house, i.e. fit cupboard locks, put make-up, shampoos etc out of their reach (remember they can climb). Although it is a good idea to let them have one cupboard in the kitchen they can empty filled with saucepans, and plastic bowls.
- Try always to have someone look after your toddler if you have to go shopping. If it is another parent, offer to take their child while they shop.
- If you are a full-time parent, try and have someone look after your toddler one or two afternoons a week so you can play being an adult again.
- Keep calm, keep your sense of humour and keep a bottle of wine chilling in the fridge to unwind with in the evenings.

Whining
Although young children still have 'young voices' discourage them regressing to whining or 'baby voices' when they want something. Crouch down so you are eye to eye and explain that you cannot understand what they are saying and would they please talk in a normal voice.

Snatching
As your toddler will have probably done very little socialising with other children they will not have come across many opportunities to need to share and the first time some other child snatches their favourite toy away may just be the first time your child whacks someone. Show them how to share by giving a toy to one child to play with for a certain time and then explaining that it is the other child's turn

with it. Find a different toy to be played with in the meantime. When the time is up ask the child with the favoured toy to pass it to the other child and make a fuss of him when he does and vice versa.

If you have children coming to your house and your child has a very special toy, ask him if he is happy for other children to play with it, although they cannot take it home or would he rather find some other toys they can play with and put the special toy away until they have left? Children are far more co-operative if they have had a hand in making the decision.

Also note that if you are visiting another child's home that favourite toy had better remain at home if your child does not wish to share it, as long as he chooses another toy to take.

Aggression – Biting, hitting and pinching

Children can demonstrate aggression by biting, kicking, hitting, pinching and throwing things. Don't worry, it is not abnormal behaviour among toddlers, but it is totally unacceptable and must be immediately discouraged.

What to do about it

If your daughter bites, hits or pinches another child, immediately tell her in your firm voice with a firm look on your face, "No, you are not to bite/hit/pinch". Firstly, ask her to apologise to the victim and check the victim is OK. Then remove her to a quiet place to sit or stand with you for a few minutes cooling-off time. Do not talk to your child during the cooling-off time (approx. two minutes), she might get to see it as one-to-one attention. Afterwards explain that it is perfectly normal for children to get angry, mummy gets angry and the best thing to do is to put your hands on your hips and say, "I am very angry", get them to practice it in front of you and then send them back to play. The hands on the hips just occupies their hands preventing them from lashing out.

If she throws something, immediately tell her, "No," and take her to pick it up and help clear up if anything was knocked over then continue as above.

Why they are aggressive

Anger and frustration – Toddlers can become angry just like adults. They are lacking in communication skills and feel they have no other ways of expressing themselves in certain situations, i.e. another child takes a toy from them.

Explain how to express their feelings when somebody takes something, they should say, "No" to their friend or come and tell you or whoever is looking after them. If you have been on holiday or away on business they can be aggressive as a type of revenge for not seeing you, again they have no other way to express themselves.

Attention – Some children even this young will realise and enjoy the attention they receive when they bite or hit. Be sure to encourage and praise more social behaviour such as playing nicely with a friend, saying please or thank you. Make sure they are getting plenty of positive attention.

Feeling threatened – If children feel overwhelmed by their surroundings or there are too many children for them to cope with they may bite or lash out as a self-defence tactic if they feel endangered. If you feel your child is finding it hard to cope in certain situations try and avoid them until he is a few months older.

Insecurity – Domestic arrangements suddenly changing can cause children to feel very unsettled and they suddenly begin biting or become aggressive. Divorce, death, even parents returning to work can trigger this behaviour. Give your child plenty of reassurance.

Too much energy
Toddlers have an abundance of energy which can build up inside them until they eventually 'blow'. To avoid this pitfall make sure they have a good run around every day and some fresh air. If they sit in front of violent cartoons all day with no exercise they may well lash out if they are asked to do something they are not so keen on.

Fear

If children feel afraid, in danger or threatened they can often misbehave to try and protect themselves. Three and four year olds start to have a sense of the world around them and this can arouse all sorts of fears. If you think this is the problem talk to and reassure your children. Never undermine children's emotions.

Copying

Some households still believe in slapping children as punishment and children from these families will automatically assume they can do the same.

If children pinch bottoms it is more likely they have seen their parents pinch each other's bottom and liked the reaction of the recipient. Mothers very often gently pinch their child's bottom, so if your child pinches someone's bottom explain that you can only do that within families.

Dealing with unsociable behaviour
5 – 14 years old

Children, whether you believe it or not, actually want to please their parents and when they demonstrate poor or unacceptable behaviour they are doing it for a reason. The trouble is they won't realise the reason themselves and it will be up to you as parents to find out what it is. Try talking to your children to see what they are feeling. It would be so much simpler if children could explain their problem. If only they could tell us, for example, "Mum, Dad, look it's like this, I've had your undivided attention for four years and now there's this new kid in my territory, in fact in my old cot. She's taking a large portion of your time and quite frankly, I'm not happy. So to vent my feelings I'm going to throw a tantrum the next time we are in a café." You don't have to be Einstein to work out that problem, jealousy, but it's finding out by trying to decipher their behaviour which is the tricky bit. However, once you have worked out what the problem is you can address the root cause and hopefully see a change in their behaviour. This may take a bit of trial and error.

Trying to decipher problems

Problem
Any behaviour that may get them noticed by their parents, shouting, jumping up down, constantly interrupting. Children usually look to see if their parents are watching whilst they are 'performing'.

Possible cause
Lack of positive attention. Some children simply do not have enough positive time with their parents and 'perform' for their attention. Other children will misbehave because the consequences when they do, gives them far more attention than when they behave well.

Solution
Basically, children have needs which are not being met.

"You must be joking," you're probably thinking, "They have TVs, videos, DVDs, CD players, bikes, Playstations and a wardrobe of designer clothes. They've got everything they could possibly want." And herein could well lie the problem. None of these are essential for happy, well-behaved children, although you may think they are. What is essential for children from their parents is regular physical contact, individual attention, respect and positive time.

Young children often interrupt phone calls or parent's talking for their attention. If you have been out working all day avoid long chats on the phone when your children are desperate to see you. Wait until they are in bed. Screen calls with an answerphone. Children will interrupt less and less the older they get. If they interrupt while you are talking to someone else, tell them firmly not to interrupt and that when you have finished talking they will have your undivided attention.

Problem
Aggression, hitting, lashing out. Controlling their temper. Truancy.

Possible cause
Parents' divorce, serious illness in the family, frustration at school through possible learning disorders or being bullied. Simple frustration.

Solution
Divorce – Although doctors are in general agreement that children are better off with one happy parent rather than two unhappy parents, the trauma of divorce takes its toll on everyone concerned. As adults, parents must put their children's well-being before their own feelings of hurt. Few divorces are

harmonious and usually one parent is far more embittered than the other, but however wronged you feel, however much you now despise your ex, never, ever, use your children as some sort of emotional pawn. They have done nothing to deserve it. Your children still love both parents and however much you want them to hate your ex as much as you, leave your children out of it. Avoid saying awful things about your ex to them or somebody else in their hearing range. It is hard enough for children when their parents separate so don't make it worse by trying to get the children to take sides. A few years down the line you may be happier than ever with a new partner but your children may carry their emotional scars for the rest of their lives. And don't make it difficult for your ex to see the children, why punish the children?

If only one good thing can come out of your divorce make it your children's smooth passage from a two-parent family to two single-parent families.

Children often blame themselves for divorce so they will need extra physical contact and love for reassurance. Depending on their ages, explain what is happening, and I don't mean, "Your father's a filthy, lying, cheating swine," kind of explanation, but a simple, "Sometimes adults don't get on any more and don't want to live together, but Daddy and I both love you very much."

Anger – Do not wait until your daughter hits her brother for the fourth time. After the first whack take her away from the action to a quiet spot to cool-off. Explain very firmly that you must never hit another person and as an immediate penalty reduce her TV time that day. Let her have a five-minute cool-off period. She must apologise to her victim, then taking hold of her hand or putting your arm around her, talk to her about her anger and try and get to the bottom of it. Just because she hit her brother does not necessarily mean that her brother is the cause of her anger.

However angry you are with children never shout, call them names or hit them. This will only teach them that they can deal with their anger by behaving in an aggressive and verbal way. Explain to your child that it is perfectly normal to get angry but they must learn to control it and perhaps the next time she wants to hit her brother to move away from the situation or to come and see you or go and hit the pillow on her bed.

Isolated incidents can be quickly dealt with but children who repeatedly show aggression suggests a deeper lying problem. Try and find out the cause of the problem by talking to them but if the aggression persists, seek professional help.

School
If you suspect there is a problem at school whether academic or social ask your child first, but if they are not forthcoming contact your child's teacher. If you suspect your child is being bullied immediately make an appointment to see the head of the school.

Illness
Depending on their age explain the illness. Try and reassure your children that everything possible is being done to help cure the patient and a home made get well card would really cheer-up the patient.

Frustration
Talk to your children about friends, school, activities and the family to try to discover the route of of the frustration and then help to dispel it.

Problem
Sudden change in behaviour, throwing tantrums, aggression towards a sibling.
Possible cause
Jealousy, change of circumstances, inferiority complex.
Solution
Jealousy – Sibling rivalry is hard to stop. Jealousy is an emotion that's not easy to just shut down however much you reassure them. As parents you simply cannot be expected to be judge and jury for all of their squabbles or treat them exactly the same because all children are individuals. Bickering siblings seems to upset the parents more than the children. Whenever I heard mine squabbling I would go in to see what was going on and sometimes they agreed they were fine. Sometimes they were not. Unless they start becoming violent just ask them to go to another room or outside so that you can't hear. If their bickering does get aggressive just separate them into different rooms and tell them to play on their own. Don't feel guilty if you find that one week you are spending more time with one child than the other. You cannot expect to have a stop-clock on sharing your time. In the end it will even itself out.

When arguments become heated, try and help them come to a compromise, something they can both live with. This is a great exercise for children as it teaches them two of life's essential skills, problem solving and negotiation.

Parents must be aware to avoid making comments such as, "Why can't you be more like your sister," or, "Your brother is so good at Maths I can't understand why you're not." Children are individuals. They do not want to be constantly judged against their brothers or sisters.

The oldest child often feels jealousy towards a new baby in the family whatever you do to try and avoid it, and in a way can you blame them? After all, for a few years they have been the centre of your universe and now another child appears and takes some of your time with them away. *Quel horreur!* Asking the older child, however young, to help with the new baby, feeding, playing and generally being more hands-on often alleviates feelings of jealousy. And always make 'special' time to spend with the older child without the baby.

> My son was born exactly two years after my daughter and I thought I had done everything to avoid any jealousy. However, one day a few months later, I caught my daughter walking into my bedroom, her brother was on a blanket on the floor, and she stepped on him as she walked over him, "Katherine, you just walked on your brother," I reprimanded, "Oh", she replied "I didn't see him." My son was quite ill as a baby and was hospitalised a few times within his first two years, so he did receive more attention than would be normal. For years my daughter was jealous of her brother (and admitted it) and once when she was about nine I was taking her to school and explaining that her brother was not going to school because he was ill, "I hope it's life-threatening," she replied (little charmer). Anyway fortunately, brother and sister are now very close.

When arguments end in tears, as they sometimes will, sit in between the two children and tell them how lucky they are to have each other, how 'only' children have no-one to play with and how hard it is as parents having to listen to their lovely children fighting with each other.

Change of circumstances

Moving house, school, new partner, new nanny, any of these changes can make a child feel insecure and can manifest itself in a change of behaviour. Once you have identified the problem extra reassurance will usually resolve it. And that does not mean just a quick word. It may take several months of spending a little extra time with them and giving the reassurance that physical contact such as a protective arm around their shoulder or a hug can give.

Introducing new partners can also arouse feelings of jealousy and conflicting loyalties. There is nothing like talking to your children to discuss the new situation. Ask them how they feel. Do they feel angry or threatened? Do your best to dispel their worries. You cannot expect children to be cock-a-hoop about their mother or father having a new partner or for their parents suddenly to want to do everything 'like a family' with the new stand-in for the real parent. It will take time and patience depending on your children's age, how long their parents have been separated and the attitude of the parents to each other.

Inferiority complex
Sometimes children will behave in silly ways to overcome a sense of inferiority, perhaps in class before a test or during PE. Not every child is going to be great at everything, so just continue to build up their self-esteem and explain that although they may not be able to climb the ropes in PE most people would love to be able to paint like them.

"Defiant, me? No!"

Problem
Defiance, protests with attitude. Ignores or takes time about carrying out requests.

Possible cause
Asserting themselves. Testing you and their boundaries.

Solution
Children will go through periods of asserting themselves in their bid for independence. As children mature they are less likely to throw tantrums, (unless you let them get away with them as toddlers) but they will make some type of stance to try and assert themselves. Children may well become defiant when asked to do something to see what reaction they receive. As children grow up the need for boundaries remain, although you will move them to accommodate their need for more independence and responsibility.

To test you

Children will sometimes misbehave to test their parents' reactions. They push the boundaries to see if they are still in place or have been moved. Parents will earn the greatest respect from their children if they are kind, firm and consistent in enforcing their rules. Their children are much happier knowing exactly where they stand.

Defiance can be shown by straightforward refusal to do something, questioning why they should do it, telling you how stupid your rules are or carrying out any request extremely slowly.

Keep calm and keep your temper. If for example, you ask your son to lay the table and he makes as much noise as possible with the knives and forks, puts them roughly on the table and walks off. Ask him to come back into the kitchen, sit at the table with him and ask why he has done such a poor job as he knows he will have to redo it.

He may say that why should he have to lay the table, his friend doesn't have to and anyway he was in the middle of his homework. Explain calmly to him that someone has to lay the table and that you share jobs out in your family. You have to do plenty of things you don't like. Yes, you can understand his feelings but it would be so much easier just to do it properly the first time. Would he prefer a more grown-up job? If he begrudgingly says, "Yes", ask him to help with the cooking the following night. Apologise to him for interrupting his homework but insist he re-lays the table. If you ask your children to do something **stand firm** until it is done and then thank them.

If your son starts kicking a ball around the sitting room, rather than scream, "Get that ball out of here. You know you shouldn't have a ball in here," tell him calmly but firmly, "You know something might get broken and you'd have to pay for it, so put it away and play with something else and I'll give you a game in the garden after lunch. Pass it to me and I'll look after it until then." If he continues to play with it and doesn't pass it to you, pick it up yourself and take it away. Explain that there will be no game after lunch and thirty minutes less TV.

Problem
Talking back

Possible cause
Anger, hurt, frustration, fear. Lack of parental respect. Asserting themselves, showing off in front of friends.

Solution
You tell your son he has to do something and he replies, "That's what you think and who's gonna make me?" Don't reply with the obvious, sarcastic, "Well actually I am," as you'll be heading for a power struggle. Ask him to join you in the kitchen or alone in another room, detach him from siblings or friends. Then ask him calmly why he is talking to you in that way and that you have never spoken to him in those tones. Insist on an apology. Tell him that it is out of character for him to speak like that as you've always got on so well and is there something worrying him causing him to behave in that way.

Treat children with respect and they will learn to treat you with respect.

If your son talks rudely to you in front of his friends don't bother trying to talk to him there and then as it will only encourage more back chat (showing off in front of his mates) but simply say in your firmest, calmest voice, "I will not be spoken to like that. There will be no TV, Playstation or computers for the rest of the day." Don't be drawn into discussion, compromise or negotiation. Carry out the punishment, he will feel a fool in front of his friends who won't be able to use the TV or computer either. When his friends have left, ask for an apology and explain that it is unacceptable to talk to his mother or anyone like that, does he understand, wait for a "Yes". Tell him the incident will be forgotten as long as it does not happen again.

Problem
Running around supermarkets or shops, playing up with their siblings when out in public.

Possible cause
Boredom, fun.

Solution
Children very quickly get bored, either having to wait in queues, waiting for mum to try on dresses, or in supermarkets. And when children are bored they will do something to relieve that boredom. It may be playing under the dress rails, annoying a sibling or running off in the supermarket, all of which will anger you.

If you simply cannot avoid taking them shopping, buy them a new comic each to look at while you are busy. In the supermarkets relieve their boredom by getting them to help. (See, How to behave in supermarkets page 124)

Problem
Tantrums, whining. Generally badly behaved.
Possible cause
Lack of parental discipline. Parents give in too easily and children have learnt that, "No" means, "Maybe" or "Yes". Behaving to expectations.
Solution
School-age children throw tantrums because they have learnt that is how to get what they want. Create enough and their parents will eventually give in. And although this trait is preferably nipped in the bud when they are toddlers, it's never too late to sort it out. Put them in their room on their own or get everyone to leave the room until they stop. Then completely ignore them. When they have cooled down, explain that they will never get what they want by that sort of behaviour and suggest what they should do in the future. Under no circumstances give in to a tantrum.

Children whine for the same reason. Firstly, tell them to talk in a normal voice and secondly, if they are whining it is because you have already said "No", explain that rules have changed and, "No", definitely means, "No". If they continue to whine, explain if they don't accept what you say they will have their TV time or allowance reduced. Be very firm.

Behaving to expectations
If children are constantly told that they are bad rather than that their behaviour is bad they will often misbehave because they feel bad about themselves, creating a self-fulfilling prophecy. Equally if children are told they are stupid, they will think they are stupid and may not try very hard at school. In these circumstances parents need to build up their children's confidence, self-respect and self-worth.

Turn your children's behaviour around
It's never to late

Relax, nobody gets it right all the time. Even if you are stressed out and at your wit's end because you have school age children who ignore your wishes, speak to you as though you are their slave and embarrass you in public with their behaviour, it is never to late to turn things around. Firstly, you are not alone and secondly, you **can** change things. It will take a little more effort in the beginning but parents will be amazed how quickly a badly behaved child can become well-behaved. Effort never translates into buying the latest toys or trendy clothes or a private education. It costs absolutely nothing except your time and the right approach.

And even though your child may at first not appear delighted at the change in your behaviour they will eventually be much happier. Well-behaved children are in fact, happier children because all their real needs are being fulfilled.

Parents who fail to set boundaries or discipline their children will receive little respect from them which becomes very obvious by the way they talk to their parents and behave.

Discuss with your partner about how you are both going to go about it. You will both need to remain kind but very firm and you will be consistent in your discipline. Even if you are the only parent in the house who handles the discipline it is important that your partner knows exactly what it is going to happen. If they are not going to help not to interfere and always to refer the children back to their mother, rather than do the 'wrong' thing.

If you are a single parent decide upon your strategy and stick with it.

Take control
The way to turn your childrens behaviour and manners around is to get back in control. You *can* do it, you *must* do it, at first it my not always be easy or fun, but it will be much more rewarding and you will all be far richer and happier for it. Then when the day arrives when someone comments on how well-behaved or well-mannered your children are, you can swell with pride and punch the air with a satisfied "Yes!"

5 – 8 years old
- Agree how you are going to start disciplining your children
- Set boundaries and consequences in place
- Be specific and crystal clear in your request
- Give yourself plenty of time

- Stay firm, calm and in control
- Do not give in

When you are ready for the first confrontation, take a few deep breaths and smile to yourself because you will be victorious. If you want your son to do something, make the request fairly simple, as in picking up his school blazer off the floor and hanging it up. Go up to him, (turn the TV off if it's on) look him straight in the eye and say in a level voice, "I would like you to.....now," your child may just continue whatever he was doing. Stop him from what he is doing, repeat the command in a firm 'I am in total control' voice, then ask him, "If you understand, say, yes". If he says, "No," explain it very clearly and calmly and ask him again until he says, "Yes". It is crucial that you do not get angry or rough with him, do not shout or lecture or let your son see any chink in your armour. Do not enter into any conversation as to why he has to do it, or if he can he do it later, or if can he go to the loo. He's just trying it on. You are in control.

When your son realises you mean business and you are not going to leave until it is done, children usually give in. Some children will hold out for much longer and some children's pride will prevent them from doing anything. If this is the case after ten minutes follow up with a firm, "Come on, get on with it then we can all get on with our lives." As this means his life too, he will be ready to back down and carry out the command. Under no circumstances help them.

When he has finished, thank him, leave and silently congratulate yourself. Well done, you are on the way to having disciplined children. The next time you want him to do something prepare to stand firm again. It will not be that long until he realises that Mum/or dad is starting to mean business and he will just have to get on with what he has been asked. However, don't go overboard with your new found power.

If your son misbehaves at home immediately tell him in a very firm, 'I am in total control' voice that his behaviour was unacceptable. Take him to a quiet spot and tell him to stand next to you for five minutes to think about it. Do not lecture or talk to him. Explain that his punishment will be reduced TV time or helping you around the house immediately, not after his favourite show or after his supper. Right now. If he returns to his poor behaviour, repeat the process. He'll soon get the message.

9 – 14 years

With this age group, communication helps to get the wheels in motion. There are a number of rules to regain control.

- Firstly, if the TV is on turn it off. Go right up to your children and ask them to come and sit at the table with you, now. Stand next to them until they have. If they are dawdling, repeat "NOW" please in a firm, no-nonsense, level voice.
- At the table, explain to them in your best firm but fair, 'I have a solution to this' voice, not a lecturing, 'I'm fed up with you all' tone, that everyone (including parents) in the house needs to make some changes for the benefit and well-being of the family.
- Discuss what your major concerns are, concentrating on unacceptable behaviour not whether their room is in a mess.
- Parents can pick only one poor trait of behaviour for each child.
- Children can each choose one trait about each parent.
- Give each person their time to speak and insist they must not be interrupted while they are speaking. I know it may sound mad but it sometimes helps if the person speaking holds something, such as a wooden spoon or CD (anything) which signifies that while it is being held no-one else can talk.
- Do not let children start airing their grievances about each other unless you want an all out war.
- Write the points down and discuss a compromise you can all agree on.

For instance you may say to your son, "I do not like the way you constantly ignore me, I find it very disrespectful." You should ask your son what it is about you that most annoys him, it may well be that you always call him for supper in the middle of his favourite soap and then shout when he doesn't respond.

To compromise, perhaps you could have supper at the end of the soap then you wouldn't have to shout as your son would obey. Your son agrees to listen more and obey.

It is important that you all say that you agree and that you will meet back in a week's time to see if things have improved and to repeat the exercise with another trait. Talking things over with older children and getting them to agree is half the battle. They feel quite grown-up that they have asserted their opinion and helped in coming to a compromise that the whole family is happy with. But be very sure that you are totally happy with the rules. Don't let yourself be a pushover and after everyone has agreed realise they are completely getting their own way.

To make things easier for your son when you want him to do something, rather than shout from the kitchen or the bottom of the stairs, walk directly up to him and ask him face to face, eye to eye, what you would like him to do and ask him if he understands. Wait until he says, "Yes." Be absolutely specific, "I would like you to take the dog for a walk around the block in the next five minutes. You will do that for me won't you?" "Yes, mum," "Thank you, darling."

The following week if you feel they have all made an effort, surprise them with a small reward.

If you realise the above approach has not worked and your son flatly refuses to do what you ask, another tougher approach is necessary. Firstly, before you ask your son to do something make sure that you have got the next hour or so free to carry it through. Go up to your son and eye to eye in a level tone ask him to do something, keep the task simple and short, don't for instance ask him to clean up his entire room. What you need to achieve is a quick victory so make it easier for everyone all round. Make sure the TV or computer is off. When he refuses, just sit with him and say you are going to sit there until he does what he has been asked. Keep a calm, level tone, don't start a lecture. After ten minutes, point out the first consequence, his mobile phone will be taken away for one day each five minutes you are kept waiting from now. Even if you have to wait an hour, wait. You can explain in a normal tone that although you have always let him get away with things in the past, it is not good for either of you to let it continue, so if he just does this job you can all get on with other things. He may rant and rave but do not be drawn into a discussion or argument. When he finally does the task, he will then no doubt storm off and slam doors, leave them alone. Do not go and apologise or try and justify your actions. If he has forfeited the use of his phone for seven days, immediately take the phone and hide it and under no amount of pleading or begging, give it back until after the seven days. Upholding the punishment is critical, your son will learn that you do in fact mean business.

Crime and penalties

All children at some point will do something that requires a quick, concise penalty to show them that certain behaviour is not acceptable and must not be repeated. To make it effective ensure the penalty is suitable for the misdemeanour, it is realistic and that it is carried out. React but don't over-react.

Try not to treat genuine accidents (however annoying) as intentional.

Penalties can take the form of cutting TV or computer time, cutting their pocket money, taking their mobile phone, extra help around the house or depriving time with their friends.

Make sure that the penalty you say you are going to give is carried through and immediate, so *never* make threats you are unlikely to keep, or threats for the future, i.e. "You're not going to get that new Playstation 2 for Christmas." Not carrying through punishments teaches your children that although you make threats you don't keep them, so basically they can get away with unacceptable behaviour.

Be practical by making sure that the penalty is reasonable and enforceable. For instance, "You're not going to watch your favourite soap for a month," is probably a bit unrealistic as it may only be enforced for one or two nights. Never use threats that will have consequences on other people, such as, "Right, you're not going to play that football match you've been looking forward to on Saturday." As not letting them turn up would be letting the whole team down.

If your child has misbehaved and is in need of a reprimand, then deal with it yourself *immediately*. Don't use the old threat as in, "Wait till your father/mother gets home."

Firstly, this is totally unfair on the parent, who as soon as they walk through the door, no doubt tired and hungry, will be expected to punish the child for some misdemeanour that happened in their absence. And secondly, there is something very unpleasant and threatening about anticipating a punishment.

Simply deal with the issue yourself, just as single parents have to.

However, it is **never** necessary to slap or hit a child and if parents ever feel so out of control that they want to they must learn to simply walk away and cool off. Parents who have slapped their children invariably feel guilty and rotten about themselves afterwards and parents who threaten and carry out "a good slap when we get home" are tantamount to bullies. Their child may have behaved very well in the interim between being naughty and getting home, the parent would certainly have cooled off but the child still gets a whack even though he probably can't even remember what he did.

One Saturday morning, a few years ago when my eldest daughter was about fourteen, I walked into the sitting room and saw her half asleep standing watching TV eating a bowl of chocolate cereal with milk. As we had a no-eating policy in the sitting room (with the new pale carpet), rather than quietly ask her to eat in the kitchen, which she would have kindly obeyed, I shouted "K-A-T-H-E-R-I-N-E!" The next few seconds passed in almost slow motion as the shock of my voice caused Katherine to jump so visibly that the entire contents of her bowl were thrown into the air. Katherine, and I watched in horror as a cascade of chocolate coloured milk and coco pops descended onto the new pale carpet. As Katherine rushed to get a cloth, I started to laugh, that sort of hysterical laughter that terrible shocks arouse and my other two children joined in. We still laugh about it to this day.

"K-A-T-H-E-R-I-N-E!"

TV, videos and computers

Is there anything TV's aren't to be blamed for?

We read so much about how too much TV can be blamed for children's low verbal skills, inability to listen, lack of exercise, obesity and now researchers are finding links to aggression. And I'm sure there is. TV and computer games are violent and graphic, although I was brought up watching westerns and I never felt the urge to massacre my fellow members of the Pony Club.

I think families fall into two categories, families that watch a lot of TV and families who seldom watch it. To expect families whose older children watch TV every evening suddenly to be restricted to two hours a night is quite frankly unrealistic. The biggest problem with TV or computers is that the screen is occupying so much time, it is restricting the amount of contact children have with their families. But do you honestly think that if the TV goes off your twelve year-old is going to rush to you, pleading, "OK, Mum let's improve my verbal skills"?

It is up to us the parents to provide the alternatives. There is no need actually to limit TV time if you are spending constructive time with your children on a daily basis. It's quite simple. Eat with your family around a table every evening with no TV and once or twice a week play a board game or cards straight after dinner. Stick to a no TV rule until the homework is finished and suddenly this combination of dinner and homework has drastically reduced the amount of TV they watch.

Keep the supper-on-your-lap in front of TV for a weekend treat not a daily ritual.

There is the argument that TV can be educational and it can be. There are certainly plenty of educational programmes available, but let's not kid ourselves, how many children do you know who watch intelligent, factual, educational programmes? Exactly. The majority watch a constant stream of American teen humour, adult based cartoons, sport, soaps and unsuitable films. Sadly, all they are likely to learn are a few new choice expletives and see sex and family violence years before they should.

> My husband and I were the gullible ones who were sold the idea of getting satellite TV by our children on the premise that they would watch the National Geographic channel, the Discovery channel and the History channel. Pah! The nearest they have ever been to watching the History channel is watching the repeat pilot show of Friends!

Young Children and TV

TV's, videos, DVD's, computers and computer games are probably the most popular babysitters in the world. Children as young as two will happily sit in front of the screen for hours and hours on end. The trouble is, it's rather too easy, too convenient.

Too much TV *can* be detrimental to young children's social development as they do need to learn verbal skills, how to listen and how to interact. TV doesn't teach children to concentrate because they immediately go into a trance like state when they are watching and it does not teach them to listen as it is too visual. If parents let their children routinely eat their food in front of the TV the children are missing out on interacting with adults and learning any social skills.

> A lady I know told me the story of one of her clients who brought her daughter into her shop one half-term. The child was about four and spoke with a slight American accent. The lady asked her client if her husband was American and had her daughter picked the accent up from him. "Oh no," the lady replied quite relaxed, "It's because she watches so many American programmes." *Hello, perhaps it's time to turn the TV off.*

TV time, like most other decisions parents must make, is mostly common sense. If parents let their very young children watch TV all day until bedtime, with little or no fresh air or exercise surely they cannot be surprised when their toddlers cannot get to sleep!

Do not let televisions just stay on all day. Young children should not watch more than two hours TV a day. Be selective. After you have watched a programme with your child, turn it off. Children love their parents to watch programmes with them, and you can then talk to them about what they saw, which encourages their speech and observation skills, plus you can explain anything they may not have understood, however simple it may have appeared to you. But children also need to play imaginary games with their toys or role play and if the TV is on they are more likely to just watch.

Obviously, TV and certainly computers have their place in today's society, but limit a young child's viewing to about 2 hours a day. Select programmes or videos for young children to watch. After that time turn it off otherwise it will start to become too much of a habit, a habit that will be hard to break. Why do you think there is a running joke about three years olds being asked by their parents to set the video recorder? It's because they spend so much time with them, they can!

Avoid falling into the trap of letting your children have a TV in their room. Because without a doubt they are going to watch more than they should. You will probably have no idea what they are watching, however unsuitable, and they will go to their rooms rather than spend time with the rest of the family. Parents put TV in young children's rooms in the hope it will keep them in bed in the evening. If these children are going to be awake for half an hour to an hour watching their favourite video, the time would be much better spent being read to or playing with a parent. The video is going to keep children awake longer than they should be because it is so visually stimulating. Research indicates that children find it harder to get to sleep if they have been watching TV just before bedtime.

If by the time your children reach fifteen and you have a good open relationship with them, they want a TV in their room to watch with friends, or because they like to be more private, then happily respond to their wishes.

TV's are wonderful babysitters when you are desperate for half an hour's peace and quiet or want some time with your partner. They can also be used as rewards, for instance, your child is more likely to get dressed for school or at the weekend if they are promised they can watch some TV as soon as they have.

The alternative

Children who are brought up being only allowed to watch television for a couple of hours a day accept it and naturally do other things. More and more families are either getting rid of their TV's or refusing to have one and they find their children are reading more, communicating with them more and performing better at school.

If you have child care at home, make sure they know exactly how much TV you want your child to watch and what programmes they can watch.But do not be conned. If they are only allowed two hours' TV a day, they will have to choose which programmes they watch. Stand your ground. Life is about choices.

How to limit TV time

Under 10's

If your children are under the age of ten simply tell them that the new house rule is only 2 hours of TV after school.

When the chorus of, "Aaahhhh Muuuum, that's not fair," has calmed down explain that each evening you are going to do something with them either a board game or cards or a role playing game or they can read, play or listen to some music. They will certainly enjoy the idea of playing something with their parents and explain that at the beginning of the week you will help them select which programmes they will watch each day so there are no last minute arguments.

If your children make noises about how you're going to watch it when they've gone to bed and that's not fair, explain that when they are your age they can sit and watch TV all day and night if they want to - that's fair.

Over 10's

This is the group where you will meet the most resistance. Sit them down around the table with a piece of paper and a pencil. Tell them the new house rules and after the predictable wails of, "Wot, that's not fair," and "You can't *doooo* that," explain that you want to spend more time doing things with them and talking to them. Perhaps you are going to start eating around the table together so the TV couldn't be on anyway. Soften this harsh, cruel blow to their lifestyle by suggesting for the first few nights you all play cards for money, which you will provide, suggest a pounds worth of 10p's each. Expect the sarcastic, "Wow! That much" and ignore it. On their piece of paper, they must write down which TV programmes they would like to watch. There will have to be a certain amount of compromise especially with children of different ages, but be firm, don't be ground down however much they think they have to watch something.

By limiting their TV watching time you now have a wonderful bribe on your hands. Your children can work towards buying extra TV time. Keeping their room tidy for a week (let's get real, three days) might buy an extra two hours TV at the weekend or an hour every day it is kept tidy. Of course, they all have to pull their weight as it would be too difficult to have the TV on for only one child. If your teenager agrees to iron the contents of the ironing basket they can do it in front of the TV. Equally if they misbehave they have their viewing time reduced. *Oh sweet joy, at last, parent power!*

As far as computers go, they can choose TV or computers for their two hour limit unless it is to be used exclusively for school work.

Swearing

Young children usually learn their first swear words from their parents or siblings. They will overhear unsuitable words said in moments of anger and frustration and then use them when they are angry or frustrated.

For example, if you're driving in your car and someone cuts you up, you momentarily forget there is an impressionable young child strapped in the back seat, and may let rip to the offending driver with something *unforgivable* along the lines of, "Can't you drive, you stupid bloody cow?"

"Children usually hear their first swear words from their parents."

A week later, you may well get a call from your child's nursery teacher requesting a few minutes of your time. In this time it will be reported that your child was overheard calling the little girl who had accidentally spilt her drink over your child, "You stupid bloody cow." Simply explain to your child that you had been very wrong to use those words and the teacher had told you off, and make an agreement that neither of you will use them again. Amazingly, being that straight-forward usually works.

Sometimes children will use swear words for attention. When this happens do not get excited and upset, as in doing so you will be giving exactly the anticipated reaction.

Just quietly ask exactly what it is they were trying to say and tell them how to say it politely. Try and diffuse a situation rather than ignite it.

As children get older, their vocabulary will become more rich and varied than you would probably prefer. TV, videos and films, are the biggest source, followed by their peers and parents. Unfortunately, most of us use expletives fairly regularly at home without even noticing it.

However, if children start swearing at home on a regular basis, do something about it. Tell them in a matter-of-fact way that if they are old enough to watch these movies which flaunt bad language, then they should be old enough to know not to use it at home. If they continue, don't rise to the bait and get angry, just immediately impose a punishment such as refusing them any TV or computer time for that day.

If your children have friends that use bad language in your home, simply inform them in a firm 'no nonsense' voice that you do not allow language like that in your house. Children will often swear more in front of their friends simply to show-off. If you overhear it, simply ask them to stop, don't be sarcastic or try and humiliate them as this will make it far harder for them to back down. Explain to them that when they are in public not to swear as it is very offensive for any one who overhears.

If your children suddenly start using foul language on a very regular basis, regardless of what you say, there may be a deeper problem. Talk to them sympathetically to find out why they are so angry and discuss how their problem can be best dealt with or resolved.

ATTENTION

We all love attention and children are no different but there is a right and wrong way to get it and a right and wrong way to give it. We have all experienced a child misbehaving and thought, "He's only doing that for attention," and, yes, he probably is.

If children are not getting enough positive attention, they will do anything necessary to try and attract some, which could take the form of whining, behaving badly, being rude, interrupting, throwing tantrums; anything in fact to attract their parent's attention. Sadly, even if parents' reaction to their behaviour is to shout and scold them, they have had the desired effect, undivided attention. We will call this negative attention.

The good news is if children receive the right amount of positive attention they will not try and gain it from behaving in unacceptable ways.

"Oops - sorry"

However, it's all about getting the balance right. Although our children need to receive positive attention on a daily basis, it is unhealthy for them to have so much attention that they grow up believing the world revolves around them. If they are given so much attention from the day they are born, all day everyday, carried from room to room, never expected to play on their own, we are creating unrealistic expectations for them in the future. Use some common sense and be realistic. Children do not need and should not expect our 24/7 undivided attention. We also have partners, parents, siblings and friends who require our attention.

Positive interaction between parents and children
• Parents and children 'doing' things together
• One to one time with both and each parent
• Talking and listening to your children
• Giving attention to good behaviour

• Avoiding unrealistic attention with very young children

How to stop negative attention

Children will soon realise in which area of their lives they get the most attention from their parents and will then repeat the same behaviour when possible. For instance, if they get shouted at and a lecture every time they jump up and down on the sofa, they will continue to do it for that undivided attention. If they fall over and cry and get a huge fuss made of them, they are likely to burst into tears at the slightest thing for the same attention.

So make sure they get plenty of attention for positive actions, being polite, not getting out of bed during the evening or playing with their friends nicely.

If there is more than one child in the family make time to have each child on their own, otherwise siblings, especially twins or children of close ages, will feel they have to compete for their parents' attention; a sort of, "I am not a number, I am a free man" plea.

How to give your children positive attention

So we've established that parents' attention is sought in a negative way if children are not getting enough positive attention.

Positive attention is time well spent with children so they don't feel the need to 'perform' for it. It involves interaction with your children and it could range from a chat together on the bus to a water fight in the sea on holiday. It is about talking, listening and enjoying each others company.

Children especially enjoy 'doing things' with their parents, so try and forget computers, TV and CD players. Below are some suggestions for good old-fashioned fun and games where you can interact, laugh and enjoy your children. This is why we had them remember?

For instance, you may think spending two weeks' holiday with your children is quality-time and showing your children attention, but if you sit on the sun-lounger and read most days your children will still not be receiving any essential positive attention and will still be behaving badly for the right type of attention.

Even a full-time mum can be at home with her children all day but still not be giving them the positive attention that they need. Unintentionally it's very easy to keep brushing children aside with comments such as, "Not now darling," "In a minute," "Mummy's busy right now," "Maybe later."

Encouragement

Children are no different from adults in enjoying praise and encouragement and as they develop and learn new skills, words of encouragement spur them on to try even harder. They absolutely love to please their parents and respond positively when they realise they have. For instance, toddlers have no idea if a picture they are painting is good or bad, so a few words of praise from a parent will boost their confidence. Children of all ages need high self-esteem so they can tackle new situations and challenges with confidence.

However, as wonderful and clever as you tell your children they are, you need to make sure they get a grip on reality. For example, as they grow up if every mistake they make or below average piece of work they do is glossed over and something positive is retrieved from the situation, they will grow up believing they are perfect and can do no wrong. This is very unfair on any child as they will find it difficult to cope with criticism in any area of their lives. Imagine the scenario in the workplace, if a boss receives a badly written urgent report, he goes ballistic, he doesn't say, "The report isn't quite what I was expecting but I like the typeface you chose."

Continual unrealistic praise can cause children to become 'adulation addicts', desperately seeking praise and unable to function properly without it.

We are preparing these children for the real world, so no, we don't want to be negative with them. We must praise and encourage them when it is appropriate, but also give constructive criticism when necessary.

Creating a childhood

How do you foresee your children looking back on their childhood when they are adults? Will it be summer picnics in the park, building sand-castles on the beach, or will they look back and only remember sitting in front of a TV and computer screen, with a vague recollection of their parents occasionally putting their head around the door?

Firstly, try not to fill every waking moment of your children's day with something organised such as music, ballet classes or French lessons and, whilst I am certainly not saying they should never learn any of these skills, they must have time to be just children. Parents need to relax around their children a bit more and to make time just to enjoy them as a family. What's more important, your family growing up very close, enjoying each other and having some real laughs or your children getting an A* in GCSE Maths at twelve?

Be realistic about expectations for your children

Children do not share our priorities about clean clothing, clean faces, time-keeping, tidy bedrooms or how important Maths will be to them. They are far more concerned about being with their parents, friends and playing. And in preference they would like their parents to play with them.

Remember to let children have time to be just children

Listed below are some suggestions for spending some positive time with your children.

Playing

Some parents will find actually playing with their young children easier than others and if you do find it difficult just forget you are an adult and come down to their level. Not every game or moment with your child has to be educational. Relax, be prepared to make a fool of yourself, (we've all had enough practice) and play with your children. Be funny, pull faces, overact, remember you were once a child and your children will reap so much enjoyment from you fooling around with them. Toddlers, for instance, love simply rolling around the floor with their parents, or go on to all fours and let your children ride you like a horse. Obviously you have to try and get them off, just make sure you move low sharp-edged tables out of the way. If they fall off and start to cry, don't make an unnecessary huge fuss, kiss them better tell them to, "give it a rub" and get back on. Don't let a 'faller at the first hurdle' stop the fun.

Funnily enough, in this age of rushing everywhere trying to fit in more and more into our already packed lives, you may well find that you enjoy playing games with your children as much as they do.

Games to play

Hide and Seek

From a very young age, children love playing hide and seek, and no matter where you live, there are always chairs, doors, TV's, etc to hide behind. If there is more than one child, help one to hide perhaps under the pillows of a bed, or behind the sofa cushions etc then help (depending on their age) the other one do the 'finding'. Best not to do this just before bed as it will get them too excited to sleep.

So when you are playing, if you are doing the 'finding', say things like, 'I'm the big hairy monster coming to get you and when I find you I'm going to eat you,' and when you find them, grab them and pretend to eat them. They will squeal with a mixture of shock and delight.As they get a little older, make it a bit more exciting and terrifying by turning the lights out and using a torch. Children love to be scared (in a safe environment).

Sleeping tigers

Get your child to lie face up on the floor or sit in a chair, and tell them they cannot move, speak or laugh, then you, without touching them, have got to make them laugh or move. This is easily achieved by making silly faces, rude noises, silly movements or pretending your about to grab or tickle them. Then reverse the process and your child has to make you move or laugh. If there are more than two of you, pair up or take turns for one person to make everyone laugh.

Sharks

The aim of the game is to try and get from one side of the room to the other without getting caught by the shark. Put cushions or folded newspapers on the floor as stepping stones. Your child or children must jump or run from one stepping stone to another to try and reach the other side, the only time they can be caught is in 'the sea' between the stepping stones. The parent playing the 'shark' moves slowly between the stones, pretending not to watch, then when the child moves from one stone to another, suddenly tries to grab the child. After a few goes let your child play the 'shark'.

Dressing-up

Children, especially girls, as young as eighteen months love to dress up, so put a few items of clothing such as hats, scarves, shoes, costume jewellery and perhaps a blouse into a box or basket and help them to dress up. Choose a room with a mirror, as even as young as this, they'll want to see what they look like. After all they are going to be big girlies one day! Let them dress you in the items as well and have a camera at the ready.

Charades

We all know how to play this as adults, but young children will enjoy it just as much in a simpler form. It can be played with just two and with or without dressing-up clothes. As your child probably can't yet read, it's best if you give them a choice of who they could mime, i.e. a naughty child, an old lady drinking tea, a dog running after a stick, someone eating an ice-cream. After they have had a go, you do a mime for them. Even if there is only two of you playing, make sure that you take turns, even if your child only wants to do the mimes. Even through this simple game, children will learn to wait their turn.

Not playing the game

If at any point in any game, a child demands that they will only play if they can do or be a particular thing, i.e. the 'mimer' in Charades, explain that it is only fair that everyone will take their turn, and if they don't agree, immediately stop them playing. If there is another child present, carry on playing with them.

It is important that the child who wanted their own way, doesn't see that everything stops because of their behaviour. If there are just the two of you, your child will probably want to play something else, but very calmly refuse, explaining that everyone has to take turns and you will play with them tomorrow when they have had time to think about it. This may or may not prompt an immediate change of attitude. If it does, the lesson may have been learnt, then agree to play three more rounds with you as the 'mimer' for the first and last. If it doesn't, then get on with something on your own. Your child will be surprised at the speed the fun you were having stopped, and will either sulk or try and get you to play something else. Explain again why you stopped playing and ask them if they are sorry they behaved in such a manner. If they say they are sorry, then suggest a story, but do not continue with the game.

Be strong, and don't give in. These seemingly mild lessons all contribute to the child growing up knowing they cannot always have their own way. Remember, however harmless it may appear to let your adorable little four-year-old have their own way, at sixteen they will be a complete pain in the neck when they expect it.

Cooking

Rather than treating them to a new video buy a children's recipe book and get them to start cooking.

Helping Mum or Dad is one of life's joys for children, so whenever you can, get your children to help. Put an apron on them, let them sit or stand on a kitchen chair near you and get them mixing, measuring or stirring. Just make sure they are not in reach of anything hot or sharp utensils. Spread newspapers on the floor to catch any spills. Don't worry about your culinary expertise, your children are not going to judge you on it (yet). They simply want to help. Making simple recipes such as rice-crispie cakes or fruit jelly is great fun for kids. Toddlers will be just as happy mixing flour and water together. Don't be fussy if they don't want to use a wooden spoon or utensil. Let them use their hands.

Even if you don't want to mix pastry yourself, buy some ready rolled dessert or shortcrust pastry, some pastry cutters and make some biscuits. Lie the pastry flat on a floured board or work surface and show your child how to cut-out biscuits using the shaped cutters. Put the biscuits on to a greased baking sheet and add some currents or chocolate drops. Bake in the oven, cool and eat. Home-made biscuits or sweets make wonderful presents for friends, grand-parents and god-parents. Simply put them in a little tissue- lined box or wrap them in some cellophane tied with a bow. Let older children choose a recipe they would like to try and give them some help if necessary.

Art

You don't have to have an artistic bone in your body for your children to have fun with paints or making things. Buy some pots of finger-paints or non-toxic paints and some white and coloured papers and just experiment with them. Apart from painting with fingers and brushes, use small sponges, scrunched up tissues and cotton wool to see what patterns and effects can be created. It is always important that you join in, motivate and encourage the activity, as children, especially young ones, will soon lose interest if you set them up with an activity then do something entirely different. As they get older, you can suggest they paint or make something in the kitchen while you are busy doing something else, but in the same room. Older children need to learn to be able to work alone but under supervision. Make collages by sticking uncooked pasta shapes on paper or pictures cut out of a magazine.

The age of your child, will gauge how much guidance you will have to give. For example, if your daughter is making a cotton wool snowman and his head is bigger than his body, and your child is insistent that is how they want it, leave it. It simply doesn't matter. It is their artistic impression.

What does matter, is that you give plenty of encouragement and praise. If your child is only three and the plasticine model of a cat resembles a blob of plasticine, who cares? To your child it's a cat. Never be discouraging about what they are doing, "That doesn't look much like a cat to me," is a sure-fire way of the child losing immediate interest. Of course, you can make subtle suggestions, as in, "I can't see the pussy cat's tail. Is he sitting on it?" This will allow your child the option of realising their mistake and perhaps correcting it, or agreeing that the cat's sitting on it. It's possible that your three year old will respond with, "Mummy, this is a Manx cat!" but let's not dwell on that scenario.

However if your twelve year-old makes a cat out of moulding clay and it looks like a blob, offer some constructive criticism.

Rainy days

As soon as children can walk, up to about the age of six they are drawn to puddles and water like a magnet, so why deprive them of such a pleasure? Get them a pair of wellington boots and a mac, and tell them that you are going out puddle jumping, and they have to run or jump over as many puddles in the park as they can. Yes they get wet, so what? They are getting lots of fresh air and using up loads of energy running around having great fun. Leave the designer outfits at home on these days and dress them in less precious clothes. Take some wet wipes, a spare pair of socks and a dry pair of shoes, if you have a longish walk home.

And if they happen to be in an area where there is likely to be mud, take a plastic mug or small plastic bucket so they can make mud pies. Don't worry about a little dirt, it helps their immune system develop.

Museums

You won't always want to get wet and on the days you want to do something indoors try a visit to a local museum. Many local museums often have visiting exhibitions on show, so even if you have been before there will probably be something new to see. Your children, whatever age, will lose interest if your are there too long, so be selective and depending on their age, explain what you are showing them.

Many children's first experience of eating out is a café and this is a very good opportunity to encourage good manners at the table. Even the most restless child can remain seated without any problems in the time it takes to have a drink and a snack and they will lap up the positive attention and praise they receive.

If you take your children to museums or art galleries they must behave in an appropriate manner. Do not let them run around, make a lot of noise or climb on seating or exhibits! If you think your children are too young or you do not think you can keep them within these boundaries do something else. It is simply not fair on the rest of the general public to have their enjoyment ruined by one or two children. If your child is behaving and then for some reason becomes upset, immediately take them outside.

The National Trust have many houses open to the public and they have made visits to them very child friendly by printing observation questionnaires for children to fill in as they tour the property. I have known the most cynical 10 year-olds actually enjoy them.

Kite flying

Unlike puddle jumping, kite flying can be as much fun for adults as children. Buy a kite, not the sort that will lift a grown man off the ground at the first gust, but a simple easy-to-use kite, then choose a windy day to go to a park or open ground and avoid launching too close to trees. As soon as it is up and flying hand it over to your child and let them fly it.

Beach summer and winter

Apart from the obvious pleasures of beaches in the summer, beaches in the winter are great areas for kids to play. With few people and wide open spaces children can still enjoy building sand-castles or football, playing with a Frisbee, kite-flying even bike-riding, depending how hard the sand is. As long as it's not raining plan a Saturday trip in the middle of the winter. Wrap up warm, pack a picnic of soup, sandwiches and hot chocolate or a portable barbecue and make a day of it. Take buckets and spades or plastic bowls for sand-castles and put in the garden spade so an adult can do some real digging.

Making camps, tents

Girls as much as boys enjoy making camps and whether it's a proper tent or a rug tied to a couple of bushes doesn't much matter. But don't expect your children to just get on and do it themselves, this is a great project for dad to get involved in. Offer them some items to help 'furnish' it, a rug or duvet for the floor, put some black bin liners down first if it is damp, some cushions and even a small table. Tell them that when they have finished playing they must help you bring everything in.

Of course, if it's raining children will have as much fun making camps in their rooms.

Winter barbecues

Although we associate barbecues with warm summer evenings, or more realistically a Force 9 gale and damp charcoal, children will enjoy them just as much in autumn and winter if you cook breakfast or lunch outside. Rather than just drag everyone out into the cold to eat, organise an activity outside such as camp building, an obstacle course or a bike proficiency course and then eat when they've finished.

Catching leaves

This is hugely popular with all ages of children and adults. In autumn simply stand under a tree in your garden, a wood or a park while someone shakes the trunk or a branch and everyone has to try and catch a leaf as it falls. Sounds easy? It isn't so offer a reward of 5p (Wow!) to anyone who can catch a leaf.

Picnics

Even during colder months the thought of a walk in the woods or park sounds much more fun if you say you are taking a picnic. Include a flask of hot drinks or soup. And take some plastic bags to sit on to stay dry. Even if you buy ready made sandwiches take them out of their plastic, cut them into quarters and put them in folded clean tea towels or napkins and put them in a basket. There is just a little bit of magic about unfolding parcels of sandwiches in cloth, which there isn't in ripping off plastic wrappers.

Watch an event
Children love just to be with one or both of their parents, so this is a great opportunity for dad and child to do something together. There will nearly always be some sporting activity happening most weekends near you, local football or rugby matches, stock or touring car racing, point-to-points, the choice is endless. Look in your local paper to see what's on.

Gardening
Children love pottering in the garden 'helping' their parents so depending on their ages give them an appropriate task. If you have the space let them grow a sunflower which will invariably grow much taller than them. Or grow a row of vegetables, your children can help you prepare the soil, plant the seeds, water them and watch their progress each week and eventually eat them.

Memories are made of this

Water fights

On a hot day in the summer, if you have a garden, get the hose out, if you don't have a hose, buy one. They're worth it. Arm each parent with a dustbin lid or umbrella as protection and they have to try and get the hose (which is on full throttle) away from their child. Take turns and as the water rides at theme parks warn: You will get wet.

With younger children hold the hose about a foot from the grass and let them jump over the water arc, or alternatively lift it up so they have to run underneath. Regardless of how young they are let them have the hose for a turn and yes, they will without doubt turn it on you.

Use empty liquid washing-up bottles for squirting water and plastic buckets for serious water fights.

COMMUNICATION

Communication is such an important factor in the family. It is essential families talk together and I don't mean the daily pleasantries of, "Good day at school?" "Supper will be ready in ten minutes," "Don't tease your sister," "Have you any homework?" and "Night darling," but really talk and discuss. It is very easy as children grow up for parents to slip into only speaking to them only when they want them to do something or to stop doing something. And with time so precious in many families, the dinner table is the one place you can all talk together. By regularly talking together children will learn to be open with their parents. Problems are more easily discussed and values are imparted. We must never under-value the importance of communication within our families.

Encouraging speech

Try and avoid using dummies. They are unhygienic, look ghastly, arrest speech development and most of the time are unnecessary. The more they are used, the more dependent toddlers become on them, until the point comes when they cry to *have* their dummy. However, in emergencies, they do have their uses. For example, if a baby starts screaming in the middle of the supermarket or in a public place, this is the perfect time to placate them with a dummy.

From as young as 6 – 7 months babies might start trying to speak. Obviously it won't be speech to us, just a series of sounds, but as far as we know our babies might be trying to tell us the rudiments of nuclear physics, so why do we stick something in their mouths to shut them up? If only we could use dummies with such gay abandon on adults.

Reading stories

Children enjoy being read stories and will learn from a young age that books are a source of stimulation and fun. Even before children can speak they will be able to understand words, so involve them with a story book by asking them to point to different things in the pictures.

When they have started to speak, encourage listening by asking them questions before you read the story so children will have to listen for the answer.

Building listening skills

I am sure we all know someone who was clearly never taught how to listen as a child so let's make sure our children never suffer the same fate. Listening is a first step to concentrating.

Encourage listening and memory skills by using simple demands.

Start with simple instructions. For example, "Please bring me your socks." When they have succeeded, gradually move on to another instruction, "Please bring me your shoes and get your coat," and then when they can follow two instructions, move on to, "Please pick up your teddy, take it to your room and put it in the toy box." Always praise them when they have accomplished a task.

When you are out in the street or in the park or in a wood stand still and ask your child to listen to the sounds they can hear and to describe them. Play different types of music at home and ask your child which ones they like.

Rather than plonking your child down in front of the TV let them listen to an audio story. Personal CD players with stories are also perfect for travelling. In cars there's no arguing between siblings which story to listen to as they each have their own and they are less likely to fight as they are occupied.

Whilst we are training our children to be great listeners we must remember to listen to them. It is so easy to brush aside comments or opinions young children have without really listening to what they are saying and then we wonder why they don't bother listening to us. So talk to them, ask what they feel about different things what is important to them. Talk about their friends, what makes them angry. Above all when they want to say something, listen to them properly. You may well be surprised how perceptive children can be.

Bring back the family meal

Why?

Ever since evolution we have been educating ourselves away from eating with our fingers and grunting. But since the arrival of fast finger foods combined with TV, video, DVD, computer games, and the demise of the family meal, we seem to have come full circle and children are again eating with their fingers and grunting. And not only do we seem to condone this kind of behaviour but we are also unintentionally encouraging it.

The breakdown of the family meal together around a table has sadly taken its

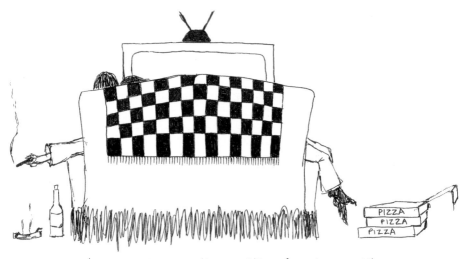

In many homes this is 'the family meal'!

toll in many ways. Firstly, children do not know how to hold conversations with adults, they are having no supervision on how to eat or behave correctly at the table, and finally, it is now suggested that the absence of the family meal is causing depression and mental-health problems.

All this because we eat pizza in front of the telly??!!

The hard facts

Scientifically based study recently completed in Spain reinforces studies that have been done in other parts of the world, which concluded that families who don't eat meals together produce children with more psychological problems than those who do. But eating as a family doesn't mean sitting around a TV with some fast food. It means sitting around a table together, sharing a meal and interacting with each other.

Sadly, the lack of family meals together has also been connected to rising crime, depression and anxieties and mental-health problems among adolescents. And we thought it was the family meal *that caused* these problems, with the over-powering father, the stressed-out mother and the arguing children.

Well, it is up to us to create a happy and harmonious atmosphere at the table, so the children and ourselves will actually look forward to this time.

Dr William Doherty, author of many books on the family, states that the time spent over a family meal is, **'crucial to a child's overall wellbeing when it comes to progressing in school.'** He goes on to say that the family meal also creates, 'a forum for bonding and warm conversation with benefits far beyond the dinner table'. And he's right.

Invaluable time

With so many parents both working, time with their children has been greatly reduced. So the family meal is the perfect way of combining talking with them, continuing their social education and really bonding 'as a family'. By enjoying regular family meals together and having the opportunity to talk, the family will become very close. Children, even with single parents, will benefit from the sense of belonging to a family unit.

Through talking and discussing things, which over the years may progress from toys to world issues, your children will get to know so much about you, your opinions on topics, what you consider right and wrong, your likes and dislikes and what you find acceptable and what you don't. In turn you will learn so much more about your children, their opinions, their thoughts and even their vulnerabilities or weaknesses. This closeness and respect that you will have for each other will considerably reduce the chance of arguments and bad behaviour as they will seldom do anything which they know will annoy you. It will prove much easier to discuss with your teenagers any issues which may arise thus avoiding head-to-head clashes.

Start having a family Sunday lunch together, invite friends with children to join you. Apart from the enjoyment factor and time to relax, this is another great opportunity to continue your children's social. Get your children to help make a dessert and lay the table.

What's the alternative?

The alternative to the family meal is eating on a tray in front of the TV, or perhaps eating around a table but again with the TV on and anyone who dares to speak is confronted with a, "Sshh". So when are you all going to talk together? I mean really talk, not just ask your children questions, which require monosyllabic answers.

What happens socially to those who have not learned to interact or eat properly around a table when they need these skills in adult life? Apart from much social life being centred around meals, business is often conducted at the table, breakfast meetings, lunches and dinner are all opportunities to meet existing and prospective clients. Anyone who does not know how to behave will be judged accordingly.

How to achieve the modern day family meal

It is very unlikely that both parents will be around early enough during the week to eat with toddlers or young children as a family, so make the effort at the weekend. Even if you have toddlers still in high chairs, eat early enough so that they can be present. During the week sit at the table with your toddler or young children while they eat, never let children eat on their own at a table, always sit and talk to them and encourage their table manners. Children are far less likely to be fussy eaters if their parents are eating with them.

When it is possible, all eat together in the evenings and depending on your children's ages and homework load, try to remain at the table after supper and all play cards or a short board game. But don't worry, just because you have started to eat and talk together as a family doesn't mean that you can't all enjoy a weekly take-away pizza with your feet up in front of the TV together.

If neither parent can be home to eat with toddlers or young children tell your nanny that she must sit, talk to them and help with their manners. (see Teaching your nanny page 152).

Single parents

Single parents can still create the family meal around the table as described. The only difference is obviously there is just one parent present. But all the advantages of being at a table together are still relevant.

When convenient, ask grand-parents, aunts, uncles or close friends to join you, so that apart from having company yourself, your children become used to talking to other adults and listening. Explain to your guests that your children will be joining them for supper. You can even give them a couple of subjects relevant to your children that they could talk about. Just make sure that you don't get so involved chatting to your friends that your children are ignored. Wait until you have let the children get down from the table before you sort the world out.

Whatever kind of terms you are on with your child's other parent, it is very important that there is continuity in their upbringing, that is to say that the child is being brought up the same way in both households. Obviously this area can be a minefield if step-parents or new partners are involved, so discuss, if you are on talking terms, or otherwise write, to explain how your shared child can most benefit from time spent in both homes.

Laying the table

Children from the age of three should be encouraged to start helping to lay the table, even if they are just putting some paper napkins on side-plates, and don't be sexist in your choice of jobs. Boys can lay a table equally as well as girls. Letting children make small decisions as in which colour napkins or candles they would like to use, will give them a sense of importance and pride. Never under-estimate how children of this age simply love to help.

By four, they can lay the table with guidance. The easiest way for them to learn is for you to lay one place setting with the cutlery, side-plate, napkin and a glass etc, and ask them to copy it at the other places. Obviously, with small children, carry the knives and glasses to the table for them and explain how to hold knives by the handle and not by the blade.

For special occasions, use a tablecloth and show your children how to be a bit creative with the napkins by tying ribbon or raffia around them. Let them put a few leaves or flowers in a vase for the centre of the table and a couple of tea-lights in small glasses. Always praise and thank them for their effort. However, as they get older, if they lay the table in a sloppy fashion, with the odd knife at right angles to the fork or if they have forgotten to put the glasses out, ask them to finish it off correctly, otherwise they are learning that unsatisfactory work is acceptable.

Laying the table is a task which young children will look forward to as it is part of the preparation for the family meal, which they soon learn is a very special time with their parents.

Always get a child, whatever age, to help lay the table and if you have more than one child, let them take it in turns. Admittedly, the eagerness to help does ebb away as they reach their teens but just insist, remember you are the parents and you are in control. You are not their servant!

The meal

Whoever is cooking should prepare something that doesn't take a great deal of last minute attention, so that the majority of time is spent at the table rather than standing at the cooker. But if the thought of having to prepare a meal and cook it sends you rushing for the bottle, prepare something simple like a salad, or buy a fresh, not processed, ready-to-cook meal. The last thing the family needs is a gin-sodden cook having a nervous breakdown or the children losing their entire set of milk teeth on the first mouthful. Stay calm, have fresh fruit for dessert, followed by cheese and biscuits. Offer children water or unsweetened fruit juice, as high-sugar fizzy drinks will make it harder for them to sit still.

But if the thought of having to prepare even the simplest meal really is unappealing, then compromise. Even a take-away can be eaten at the table with a knife and fork. Your children will still benefit from all the advantages of sitting at a table with you.

Relax

The key to a happy time at the table, which is the most beneficial for the children, is for the parents to be relaxed, happy and getting along. So don't bring up any issues that might spark an argument. Steer clear of controversy. If siblings are likely to squabble, do not let them sit next to each other.

Encouraging speech at the table

This is the perfect opportunity to encourage verbal skills, eye contact and actually to talk to each other. But you must do exactly that, talk to each other. There is no quicker way for any child or teenager to lose interest than if they are being ignored, not unlike us, actually. So think about what you could talk about at the table to include the children, whatever age they are. Obviously, this becomes easier the older they get. But it is so important even for little toddlers to start interacting with adults at the table. Even at that age they have thoughts and opinions. And listen while they are speaking and appear interested. Try and ask questions that do not require a one-word reply and encourage them to join in and to feel confident about joining in.

Toddlers find it very difficult to sit still for any length of time, so while they are still so young, let them sit down when the food is on the table. However, when they have finished, keep them at the table with you until you have finished or are happy for them to get down. French, Italian and Spanish toddlers can learn to sit at the table, so I'm sure ours can. If children always get down as soon as they have finished, they will expect to in restaurants, which is a big no no. They should always wait to be told to get down from the table or ask, but if they do ask and you are not ready for them to leave, simply say no. Try not let them get into a habit of getting down and returning for a dessert.

Tell stories

Young children always enjoy stories about other children, especially other children being naughty, or something naughty or funny you or your partner did as a child, then ask them what they think your parents thought or did about it.

All children and teenagers enjoy telling anecdotal stories especially if they are amusing and they receive a good response, so encourage your children to recount something that happened to them, funny or otherwise. The fluency of the story will depend on their age and vocabulary, and young children may need a little prompting or help with theirs. Look at them and listen attentively. After all it's very demoralising for a child, even an adult, while recounting a story, to watch their audience rapidly losing the will to live. Keep interested, keep eye contact and never interrupt them or their siblings with table manner reminders mid-speech.

Asking them questions about their story will make them feel important and it will begin to develop their confidence in talking with adults.

As they get older teach them that if they are talking or telling a story to more than one person, to have eye contact with everyone, not just one person, thereby engaging everyone who is listening.

Praise at the table

Once or twice a week think of something your children have done that day or at school which was worthy of praise and tell everyone about it. If there is more than one child, make sure you do it for both. Children, not unlike adults, bask in praise and it gives them confidence and encouragement to go on to greater things. However, never bring up an incident that will cause embarrassment. If something has happened during the day, which has to be addressed, deal with it on a one-to-one basis, but never at the table.

Never humiliate your or anybody else's children, especially not in front of other people. Even little incidents about your child which may seem amusing to you, may be horribly embarrassing to your child when recounted over the dinner table. Children are far more sensitive than you might think.

If it's appropriate, discuss where you might take your next family holiday (without arguing about how much it will cost), or talk about an upcoming family event, or what they would like to do after supper or at the weekend. Discuss books, films, TV programmes, the news, anything to encourage conversation and opinions.

It is very important that your children look forward to these meals. To be honest, they will probably look forward to them far more than you, as you will have the unenviable task of making conversation and looking interested while toddlers extol the virtues of Lala the Telly Tubby while you're simultaneously trying to instil good table manners in them. But as time goes on you will thoroughly enjoy this time with your family, seeing how your children's thoughts and opinions change, their vocabulary increases and their table manners improve!

Laughter is the best medicine
Many over-stressed parents only seem to relax and have a good laugh when they are away from their children, yet laughter is very bonding. Try and have a laugh at the table every day together and not at the expense of someone. It works wonders for unwinding and relationships.

Encouraging listening
Once children are confident enough to talk with a group of adults and other children, they can become so enthusiastic as to keep interrupting. So now you've got them talking, they must realise when they can and can't talk. No-one said life was going to be easy!

Simply explain that everyone has to have their turn to speak and they must wait for theirs and that they too, must learn to listen to what others are saying, so they can ask questions or give their opinion if appropriate. There will also be times at the table when you may wish to discuss a subject with your partner and the children may have to sit quietly for five or ten minutes. If they interrupt, clearly explain that they can listen, but they are to be quiet and not interrupt. Although we need to interact with children at the table they must realise that life does not revolve around them. Please don't be the type of parent who stops all adult conversation as soon as their child wishes to speak, unless it is of life-threatening importance, as in, "The house/sitting room/your hair/shoe cupboard is on fire!"

Teenagers

Teenagers seldom want to talk about their school day or how their work is going, so talk about their interests or bring up an issue that's in the news and relevant to them. Ask their opinions and encourage them to justify them. Discuss fashion and tell them some of your worst fashion and hair moments. That'll certainly raise a laugh and don't get upset when they point out that you're still having them. Teenagers have got plenty of opinions and plenty to say so make sure you present them with an opportunity to be able to talk and discuss.

Table manners

The object of table manners is not to demonstrate the most sophisticated knowledge of table etiquette, but to behave with a certain poise and graciousness and to use knives, forks and spoons efficiently with ease and confidence. Let's face it appalling table manners can actually put other people off eating their meal.

Teaching table manners

Family meals can soon become a time of misery for all concerned if the child is constantly being told, "Don't speak with your mouth full," "Hold your fork correctly," "Sit up straight."

Each meal time, decide which parent is going to help with the manners. This gives one parent a break and the child is not constantly being prompted by both parents.

Young children will still need help to use their knife and fork to cut up food. Rather than keep telling them to hold their knife and fork correctly, without stopping the flow of conversation, simply put their fingers in the right position over the implements. Nearly all children, if they have been shown from a very young age how to eat properly, will do their best to achieve it. So if you see them eating nicely, praise them, tell them how grown up they are. It will encourage them to do even better.

If for example, they are eating with their mouths open, or slouching etc, catch their eye and mimic what they should be doing. They'll soon catch on.

Obviously, sometimes they will have to be told some things, but try and be positive in your advice, such as 'Instead of leaning across people, darling, just ask them to pass the peas/butter/gravy etc'. But say it in a normal tone, so that they don't feel embarrassed, or reprimanded. Table manners are just another learning curve.

Sitting at the table

When you are ready to eat, sit your children where you want them to sit, i.e. next to you or your partner or a teenager if food has to be cut up and apart from a squabbling sibling. They should sit upright and squarely on their chair with the chair pushed in close enough to the table so that they can reach their plate easily. Sitting upright will also aid digestion.

They can put their napkins onto their laps, or have it tucked in to their collar, depending on their age, or what they might be eating. The temptation to play with their cutlery or put their elbows on the table is enormous so try to dissuade them from doing so, but this habit will subside as they get older.

If they are passed a basket of bread, they should take one piece if they wish and only touch that one piece, then say thank you. They must put the bread onto their side plates. If they take some butter, they should put it on their side plate before applying it to a piece of bread. The same applies to jams and spreads.

Explain to them that it is polite to wait until everyone has their food before you start to eat unless told otherwise.

When are children ready to use a knife and fork?

Children will develop dexterity skills at different times, but they are usually ready and willing to start learning to use a child-size knife and fork by two and a half to three years. But whenever you do start, if you can see that your child is really not coping and becoming anxious, leave it for a few months.

How to use a knife, fork and spoon

This is for right-handed children. Just reverse for left-handed children.

Show them that the fork is held prongs facing down in the left hand with the forefinger resting on the bridge and their knife is held in the right hand, blade down with the forefinger on the top of the handle. Explain and demonstrate to them how their fork is used to hold the food in place while the knife is used in a sawing action to cut through it. The knife and fork should not be used to try and

tear the food apart. Cut off only a small piece of food at a time. Eating a modest mouthful is far easier to cope with and certainly more pleasant to look at.

During the meal, especially if they are talking or about to take a drink, they should put down the knife and fork (prongs facing down) and rest them on each side of the plate. Explain that they should never gesticulate and wave or point with either implement and (*please, please*) never eat off a knife.

When they have finished eating they should put their knife and fork together straight down the middle of the plate.

Teach them to hold a spoon by resting the arm of the spoon between their forefinger and thumb and grip and not to hold the spoon or any utensil like a shovel. If they have a dessert spoon and fork, to hold the fork in the left hand in the same manner, it is used to aid food onto the spoon, not to actually eat from.

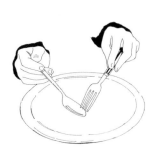

Show them how to hold a soup spoon in their right hand like a dessert spoon and to sip the soup (quietly) off the side of the spoon and the plate tilted away from them. Its perfectly acceptable to let children break off a few pieces of bread and put them into the soup, but not to let them dip whole pieces in and them try and eat the soggy slice with their fingers.

Explain to your teenagers that if they are invited to a formal dinner and they are faced with a series of knives and forks on each side of the plate, to start at the outside and work their way to the centre with each course.

Demonstrate to your children how to eat the following two favourites:

String type pasta - (spaghetti, linguine etc) They should hold the fork in their right hand and a dessertspoon in their left, (just like for desserts but the other way round) and take a few strands of the pasta. Then putting their fork in the spoon start to turn the fork to roll up the pasta. The spoon will aid the rolling process hopefully ending up with a manageable mouthful. The secret is not to start rolling too many strands.

Peas or baked beans - Ah the good old peas! Left to their own devices children will turn the prongs of their fork around and shovel them in. Try and encourage them to just squash their peas onto their fork (prongs facing down) or use the aid of another food on the plate, such as a potato to mash them into.

General politeness and courtesy at the table

That age old rebuke, to eat with their mouth closed and not to talk with their mouth full, is still as important now as it ever was. However, rather than the order, "Don't eat with….." try the slightly more cajoling, "Remember to eat with….".

Explain to your children always to ask for things to be passed to them, rather than reach across other diners' space to get it for themselves. If they are asked to pass something they should not help themselves to it first before they pass it.
If they are helping themselves to some potatoes for instance, firstly not to take too many, and if it is a second helping and there are not many left, to ask who else would like another one before helping themselves.

Regardless of their levels of efficiency with knives and forks please don't let children eat with their fingers.

When they have finished, they should thank the cook for the meal and to try and remember to compliment on all or part of the meal (obviously without encouraging dishonesty). Hopefully, if there is another adult at the table they may make the first compliment and then the children can follow.

Children should always ask if they may leave the table and when they do, if they have tried hard with their table manners and been good company, point it out, praise and thank them.

Clearing up

At home always insist that even young children take their own plates to the sink and show them how to scrape them clean before loading the dishwasher, if appropriate, or stacking them next to the sink. If you have more than one child, let them take it in turns to lay the table and clear it. As they get older, teach them how to wash-up and dry, including saucepans, put food away, clear and wipe down kitchen surfaces. Clearing up can be accomplished very quickly if everyone gives a hand, so make sure they all help.

Teenagers

The more you get your children to contribute to the household, the more they will expect to do it. However, if you suddenly start asking your teenager to lay the table or wash-up, with no previous 'helping' experience, be prepared to be confronted with a distorted, bewildered expression accompanied by an incredulous grunt of, "Wot?"

Stay calm and explain that from now on they are going to contribute to the housework. It is never too late for them to start helping, although you will have to guide them through their first few attempts. Anything not washed up well enough, goes back for them to do again. Rather than start a monologue of why they should help more around the house, (because it may be your fault for never making them as they grew up), talk about current events or films. Again this can be good talk time with children, whatever age. Of course, if you have more than one teenager, once they know what to do, they can do it together without your help, and remember if they don't finish it off properly as in wiping down the work surfaces and around the sink, back they go. One day they may just thank you for making them do a job properly. One day. I wouldn't hold your breath.

ROUTINE

Toddlers thrive on consistency. They need to know and anticipate what is going to happen. For example, toddlers will be happier if they have a routine such as getting up at a certain time, have breakfast, have some playtime, nap, lunch, walk in the park or outing, nap, tea, bedtime routine, bed. That is why toddlers love to watch the same video over and over again because they know what is going to happen and they look forward to it happening.

Regardless of how mundane such a routine may be, toddlers and young children feel reassured by it, so a sudden change to their normal routine can cause anxiety which may manifest itself in changes of behaviour.

CONTINUITY

Again children are creatures of habit. They feel comfortable with what they know whether it be school or their child-minder, so try not to disrupt their lives with too much chopping and changing which can be disturbing. Sometimes change is inevitable for all sorts of reasons, and under these circumstances children will need as much continuity as possible in other areas of their lives.

They will also respond to the continuity of being taught something regularly in the same way, for instance table manners. The speed at which they respond and learn will differ from child to child, but the more regular and repetitive the lessons, the quicker it will be.

CONSISTENCY

Older children also thrive on consistency. If a child does something wrong both parents should react in exactly the same way every time. Failure to be consistent can result in more situations where children go running to the lenient parent after being told off by the other, which is very damaging to the child/parent relationship and the parents' own relationship.

This situation can become a serious problem if parents separate and then try and gain advantage over each other by playing an over-indulgent role with their child.

How to avoid tears before bedtime (everyone's)

After children's bedtime, the evenings should be exclusively adult time, child free zones, parenting over for the day. Pick up the toys and child detritus and enjoy this adult time in peace, whether it be with your partner, friends, the newspaper, radio, TV, a book or whatever.

But for many parents just when everyone's tired and emotional, the battle of bedtime comes around. I am sure we all know someone who has a toddler or child that is constantly getting out of bed once they have been kissed goodnight. They ask for just a few minutes, or another drink, or some other excuse and then they are put back to bed, only to appear ten minutes later, more often than not the parents finally cave in and let them stay up. The scenario of the child getting up and being cajoled back to bed can last up to three hours every night. It is extremely tiring and irritating for the parents and the child is depriving itself of valuable sleep and may wake tired and bad tempered (not unlike the parents).

Establish a good bedtime routine with toddlers and you will not have a problem as they get older. Give in to them as toddlers and they will still be getting out of bed when they are ten.

Why do toddlers keep getting out of bed?
Literally because they can. As soon as toddlers are walking they want to use their new found freedom. They also want to be with their parents all the time and resent being excluded from them.

Setting bed and nap times
Set bed time and day nap times and be sure to stick to them, so that your child's body clock will begin to anticipate the sleep and wake periods.

If they are still asleep in the morning at their usual wake-up time, then wake them up, otherwise they will not be ready for their mid-morning nap and it will put their sleep and wake patterns out of kilter for the entire day.

Establishing a bedtime routine
The following is a normal straightforward routine which should be performed at the same time in the same order each evening. You may wish to add a song or a game to your routine, but whatever you do, do the same every evening and this predictability will be the trigger for your child to start relaxing.

Toddlers are great dawdlers and although you may have established a routine, they will take their time about starting it. Give your child some options to let them feel in control. For example, 'Would you like to clean your teeth first or wipe your face?' 'Would you like to wear the red or blue pyjamas?' 'Would you like to go to bed now or in five minutes?' Once they have made their own choice they are less likely to renege on it. On no account let them stay up for another few minutes, even if they beg and plead or throw a tantrum. If you give in to their request you will hear it again and again. Be firm the first time and nip it in the bud.

A relaxing bath

This is an ideal way for parents, especially working parents, to spend some relaxation time with their child. Fill the bath with warm water and baby friendly bubbles (i.e. nothing that will irritate their skin) lower the lights and light some aromatherapy candles, out of your child's reach. Put on some restful music, and even pour yourself a glass of wine, (use a plastic wine glass if you have a tiled floor, otherwise picking your way through broken glass holding a young child may not be the relaxation you had in mind). Scene set, put two towels to warm (if possible), then lie back and enjoy it with your child. Talk to them about their day and tell them about yours. It is not necessary for your child to fill the bath with every bath toy just allow one or two.

If, however, your child is not very keen on having a bath, and the very mention of the word may cause upset, leave it out. Toddlers can go through phases of not liking baths, so rather than a confrontation, just wash their face and hands, or let them do it themselves. After the bath dry them and put them straight into their pyjamas.

NB Never leave a baby, toddler or young child unattended in a bath, even if you think you are only going to be out of the room for a second.

Cuddle and story

While they are still in a cot, have a favourite chair or place to read to them, and use the same place each evening. If they are in a bed, sit with them on their bed, get them to cuddle up to you with their favourite soft toy and a drink of warm milk while you read a story. The body contact is so important. It is both calming and reassuring.

Lower the lights and ask other siblings to leave the room if you think they may

distract them, but if they wish to listen to the story then let them. You should be trying to create a calm, peaceful atmosphere, conducive to sleep.

My husband used to always lie down on one of the children's beds to read them a story or give them a cuddle. When I used to go and kiss the children good night I would often find him fast asleep on the bed while the children were sitting up laughing, thinking it was hysterically funny that Daddy had fallen asleep while they were still wide awake.

Warm milk

If your child is not allergic to milk, a warm drink in the evening will help promote drowsiness. Milk actually contains tryptophan which helps the brain to relax and serving it warm, raises the body temperature to trigger a slowdown response. If they have not finished it by the end of the story, take it away, otherwise they may become dependent on it for falling asleep.

Bed

At the end of the story put them straight into their cot or bed. Tuck them in, a final kiss and tell them that you do not expect them to get out of bed and leave the room. No discussions, no extra stories, no exceptions. This may sound tough but it will save you years of anguish. It is much more fun for your children if *you* suddenly tell them you are going to read an extra story because they were so well behaved at supper, for instance.

Learning to fall asleep

It is very important for babies and toddlers to learn to fall asleep for themselves and not be dependent on being rocked, or sung to or listening to a certain CD to doze off. Otherwise when they wake in the middle of the night, they will not be able to settle themselves back to sleep without their 'aid' and will cry for you.

Crying

If toddlers start to cry when you put them down for the night or wake in the middle of the night and start to cry, wait a few minutes to see if they stop. If the crying continues and they are genuinely upset, then go and see to them. But try to resist the urge to rush in immediately, as it may well be unnecessary and will just teach them you will be there every time they squeak.

Make sure they are tired

As obvious as this may sound, it is much easier for children of all ages to go to sleep when they are tired. And what makes a child tired? Exercise and fresh air. So try and make sure that your child gets plenty of fresh air and exercise everyday. Most toddlers will have a burst of activity early evening for up to one hour. Start the bedtime routine after it.

Creating bad sleeping habits

TV

Sitting in front of the TV for several hours will not tire your child. In fact, as soon as you say it is time for bed, all their unspent energy will suddenly surface, and they may expend it by jumping out of bed and running to you for the next three hours.

Children should not have a TV in their bedroom. Parents who think that their child can fall asleep to their favourite video are doing an injustice to their child. A video is far too visually stimulating, and the child is on their own at what can be a very bonding part of the day.

Resisting 'just a few minutes'.

If they get up and come and see you immediately take them back to their bed. In the evening when you are tired and sitting down relaxing, there is always a great temptation to let them sit with you for 'a few minutes.'

Resist this urge at all costs.

You will be creating a nightmare situation for yourself as your children will very quickly learn that it is acceptable, exciting, great fun and they will make it a habit as soon as possible.

Once children are in the habit of 'coming to see you' in the evening, they will be indiscriminate about when they come. And however much you love your children and their company, you need time on your own or with your partner. Your friends will not appreciate being invited over for an adult supper or dinner, then have to put up with your young children joining them, whatever they say.

The temptation to let them have 'just 10 more minutes' is much worse if you have been working all day. You may feel your child has got up as they don't see enough of you, you feel guilty as you don't see as much of them as you would like. And they look so scrummy and gorgeous in their pyjamas. But as long as you spend constructive time with your child when you get home, the bedtime rules must still apply.

Children who keep getting out of bed can seriously curtail your evenings entertainment

Before they have had time to crawl onto your lap, take them back to bed. If they get up again, take them straight back. Be quite firm that you do not expect to see them out of bed again. You can sometimes hide just around the door and spy on them and as soon as you see them starting to get out, appear and firmly tell them to get straight back. This pre-emptive approach can be very successful.

To avoid them using any excuses for getting out of bed, make sure they have a drink by their bed, they've been to the toilet and are comfortable. If children come down and get upset because they have had a nightmare, take them straight back to their bed and calm them down and reassure them. If nightmares persist they may be anxious about something, so look for problems at school.

When children wake in the middle of the night and come into your room, the temptation is to let them into your bed, but again resist the urge, take them back to their bed or they'll end up sleeping with you every night. If they have been upset by a nightmare, lie with them on their bed until they fall back to sleep. Let them come into your bed for a cuddle in the morning and at the weekends if you are reading the papers and having a lie in. But make sure they stay the entire night in their own bed.

The benefits are two-fold. Your children will wake in the morning well rested, as their sleep pattern has not been constantly interrupted and they have had a full nights sleep, and you have had an adults only evening and feel well rested, human and are really looking forward to seeing your children.

Overtired
Babies and toddlers find it very difficult to settle or stay asleep if they are overtired, so make sure they are getting enough naps during the day.

Effects from sleep deprivation
Research indicates that one in five children are not getting adequate sleep **which can compromise children's health, academic achievements and mental health.** In young children it can apparently harm neurological development and contributes to poor behaviour. So to avoid these horrific consequences remove TV's, Playstations and computers from children's bedrooms or ban their use at bedtime and establish a proper bedtime routine.

Toddlers refusing to go to bed

Few toddlers will gleefully run to bed as soon as they are asked, even with a good bedtime routine, so be prepared for a defiant look with a firm, "No." Now there are two ways this scenario can go, the painful, triggering a tantrum and the not so painful.

1) The painful.

You can insist they go to bed, wherein they will stand their ground even more. This no-win war of words will invariably end with the parent exercising physical strength over the child by picking them up and carrying them to bed, with much screaming and kicking (just by the child we mean), which will upset both the parent and the child.

Or you can use some reverse psychology.

2) The less painful

After the child has said, "No," say that you are going anyway. If the TV is on turn it off. Say you are going to find something in their room. And leave, don't look back, don't invite the child to come with you. If your partner or another child can join you, even better.

Go into their room and find a book, sit on the floor reading it, make noises and laugh, so your child can overhear you, and in a few minutes your child will be by your side. Children are no different from adults. They simply a) love to think they've got their own way, and b) can't stand the idea of someone having more fun than them. Can you blame them?

So now you have them in their room without any fuss and you have a book in your hand, ask if they would like the same story as you are reading, or would they like another story. And while they are deciding, you lift them into bed and read to them. If they start playing up, immediately distract them, by becoming distracted yourself (and ignoring them for a few moments) with something in your pocket i.e. an imaginary mouse, or an imaginary spider on the wall. These children are only two, they are not rocket scientists (yet) and they are easily distracted. Use this to your advantage. Use your imagination.

What to do if your child (5 to 10 years) is already getting out of bed each evening

As soon as they appear take them back to bed, however much of a fuss they kick up, put them back into bed and tell them you expect them to stay there. If they appear again, do exactly the same, don't lecture or over react. Tell them that if they stay in bed all night from now on they can watch 15 minutes more TV tomorrow or have a chocolate bar, if they get up again they will have 15 minutes less TV tomorrow. Ask if they have fully understood what you have said, "Yes," or, "No." If they say, "No," explain again. Do not let them engage you into negotiating a different reward or punishment or talking about anything else. Stay calm and firm.

If they say they cannot get to sleep

Keep them in their beds and ask them if they are worried about anything, it could be an upcoming test at school, homework not finished, a fall out with a school friend. Work out a solution with them to their problem.

Ask them if they would like to listen to a soothing CD. Once children are five years- old they are not going to become dependent on sleeping aids and calming music is simply helping to relax them. If they are really wide awake tell them they can read but they cannot get out of bed.

> When my daughter was about four years-old she would sometimes complain that she could not get to sleep so I used to tell her to try and keep her eyes open all night. She was often asleep within fifteen minutes.

EXAMPLE

Children will learn far more by watching and listening to their parents than from what they are told by them. As parents, we are the role models for our children so we must ensure that the example we set is a positive one and the way we behave in our life will be acceptable to us when they copy.

Our children will learn more by observing our values, attitudes, reactions and behaviour than by any other means. We are role models for our children whether it's a good or bad example we are setting. A teacher once said to me, "You realise why some children have problems when you meet their parents." So make sure you are not the problem.

Teaching right and wrong

Honesty doesn't necessarily come naturally and why should it? We have to teach children the difference between right and wrong just like everything else and the easiest way for them to understand your morals and values is by setting a good example.

Stealing

The thought that our little darlings may one day steal fills us with horror. None of us want our children to steal anything from anyone ever, but in reality sometimes incidents do happen. Although the very thought terrifies us that this will be just be the start of a life of hardened crime, most children who are dealt with effectively will seldom re-offend. It is vital that parents react immediately but don't over react.

Teaching ownership

It is a good idea to have a family rule that everyone, including the parents, must ask before taking something that belongs to another member of the family and to return it to them when they have finished. This teaches children to understand ownership, the concept that some possessions belong to other people. Most children's first word after 'mum' or 'dad' is 'mine!'

Close family relationships
Children from families who share a very close relationship i.e. eat together, play together, discuss topics together and are open with each other are far less likely to do anything against their family's beliefs and wishes.

Taking things that do not belong to them – the under 6's
Under 6's don't steal as they don't understand what it is. However, they may well take something which is not theirs.

Depending on how much you have explained about right and wrong to your children by this age, some children will have a better grasp of what they should or should not do.

Children up to the age of 6 have little understanding of private ownership and as some parents may have given them everything they want anyway up to this age, young children can hardly be blamed for taking what they feel is rightfully theirs. Even if they have not been totally spoilt they may well take something that isn't theirs simply because they want it with no thought that their actions may be dishonest or frowned upon and let's not forget that toddlers believe they own the world anyway.

The little darlings also take things in shops. They see us helping ourselves from supermarket shelves, so why shouldn't they? They don't understand the concept of paying at the checkout so everyone needs to be vigilant to prevent having to return shame-faced to the shop to return the jar of Nescafe that appeared in the pushchair.

Solution
As soon as you realise that your child has something that does not belong to them, firstly establish where they got it from if you don't already suspect. Take the object in your hand and ask them in a calm voice where they got it. If you immediately get angry they will be confused and probably not want to tell you. Once you know who to return it to, explain that it does not belong to them and it is wrong to take other people's things and try and get them to empathise about how upset they would be if someone came and took their favourite toy.

When you return the object ask your child to hand it over personally and apologise. Then praise them.

School age children

From the age of 6, children should understand the concept of ownership and know that stealing is wrong. However, this does not mean that they will never take anything. Children may steal at different stages of their school years for different reasons.

Reasons why children steal

Parents setting a bad example

Children will learn their values on honesty from their parents' example whether it be a good or bad one.

Let's face it, we know that being brought up in a home where parents are dishonest and constantly stealing from shops, their workplace or participating in benefit fraud is hardly going to be conducive to children growing up to be upright and honest citizens. Even if these households try and hide their dishonest actions from their offspring, their children have eyes and will soon suss out what is happening. Children from dishonest families will sometimes steal just to impress their wayward parents.

Although the majority of us are not dishonest, we must be careful that we do not send mixed messages to our children. Parents may unwittingly be teaching their children that it is OK to take things by setting a bad example.

For instance, if the local newsagent gives a parent too much change and outside the shop the parent says, "Oh, she's given me a pound too much," and keeps it, this teaches the child, it's OK to have what is not yours. The parent should immediately explain to her child that she has been given too much change and that she must return it to the shopkeeper, otherwise it would be stealing (the meaning of stealing may have to be explained). The child will also learn from the grateful/relieved/amazed attitude of the shop-keeper that this was the right thing to do.

Prevention

Children will learn their values from you. Honesty, is a valuable topic to discuss around the dinner table. Tell them that some families perhaps do not view stealing with the seriousness that your family does. Let your children know that stealing is unacceptable in your family. Explain to them how appalled you are that people can behave in that way, and ask their opinions as to why they think people do commit crimes.

Depending on their age talk about incidents that could happen at school or real-life crimes (perhaps currently in the news) including theft and fraud. Children will invariably ask what your reaction would be if they committed a crime and rather than tell them what they're anticipating, which is threatening harsh punishments and a life on the streets, explain how terribly disappointed, ashamed and let down you would feel. You will almost see them thinking angering their parents is one thing but hurting them is quite another.

To get what they want
There will always be some child at school who will have too much pocket-money, too many toys, too many sweets and will flaunt them in front of their classmates which can create envy in the classroom. If children have no allowance they may feel they have no way of ever 'competing'.

Prevention
Allow your children a small amount of weekly pocket-money when they start school and teach them how to use it. Even from this age they can start to learn the value of money, so help them how to budget for the week and not to blow it all as soon as they get it *(if only we'd all had that lesson!)*. If they want a particular small toy, explain that they will have to save towards it and perhaps do some extra chores around the house to help pay for it. However, they may as well as learn from as young as possible that they simply can't have everything they want, no matter how many chores they do or how much they save up. Explain that we, as parents, can't have everything we want and sometimes we just have to settle and be happy with what we have.

Peer pressure
Children will often steal as a dare to prove themselves worthy of a certain peer group or just to show-off to them.

Prevention
Children who feel they are not worthy of their peer group are suffering low self-esteem and will need plenty of encouragement and praise to become more

confident individuals. Invite different friends of your child to your home to help them develop new friendships.

Seeking attention
Some children steal for attention and to be noticed. These children often lack self-esteem and perhaps have problems at school and receive little attention at home. Although the attention they will receive from their actions will not be the type of attention they would prefer, it will still be attention. It is almost if they are silently crying out, "Will somebody please notice me."

Quite often second siblings may take things in rivalry for the attention they perceive the first-born is getting.

Prevention
As said above, children with low self-esteem need plenty of encouragement and praise to become more confident.

If children are stealing for attention they probably already know that it is wrong and it will be going against their parents' wishes but it will certainly get the attention they crave.

Parents of children lacking attention will have to re-examine the positive time they are giving to their child and whether they are at home all day or working, the time they do spend with their child is effective.

Because they can get away with it
Although parents should not over react to children stealing, equally they should not under react. Taking little or no action will hardly be putting out the message that they are never to steal again.

There was a recent case of a teenager who had been injured by the victim of a robbery he was committing and his mother when interviewed said, "He didn't deserve to get hurt, he's not a bad lad, just a bit of a rogue." Surely, we all want to cry out, "*Madam, wake up, your son is not a bit of a rogue, he is a dishonest, law-breaking thief who was trying to steal someone else's property!*" But while parents adopt that type of attitude to their children's dishonesty, their behaviour is not going to change.

What to do if your child steals

When a child is caught stealing, action must be taken immediately. If there is no question that the child is guilty, the parents must adopt a very firm matter-of-fact tone of voice. **Never** shout or scream as this will signal to your child that you have lost control and whatever you say will be less effective.

If a chocolate bar or bag of sweets was taken from a shop, parents should take their child back to the shop and return the said article (if it hasn't been eaten). The article will have to be paid for which will either come out of the child's allowance or they will have to work around the house to pay it off. As well as a spoken apology to the shop-keeper, parents should insist their child sends a written apology.

Parents must then sit down with their child, one-to-one, no nosy siblings listening in, and ask them why they did what they did and did they realise how wrong it is and how lucky they hadn't been caught by the shop-keeper and the police called. Parents should not walk up and down giving the, "What shame they've brought to the family, how could they after all that's been done for them," lecture and avoid name calling. However, it is important that the parent talks to their child in a 'concerned let's discuss this' tone and not an 'I understand everything' tone. Children must realise that they have done something very bad but they must not be made to think that they are bad people, as this can lead to far worse problems.

Whatever the child says and whatever excuses they give for their actions, they must not be let off the hook. Parents must explain that the child can always come to them with any problems, no matter what it is; that there is nothing that cannot be discussed. Ask them if they realise the seriousness of taking other people's belongings, and get them to promise they will never do it again.

Some type of penalty should also be enforced such as no television or computer time for two days, or not being able to see friends at the weekend. It is very important that the punishment is upheld otherwise your credibility is undermined and the seriousness of the misdemeanour trivialised.

Parents should also consider whether they have been too busy to give their child any attention recently, or if there have been any changes in their lives that may have caused the problem. However, do not offer excuses as this will only negate your disapproval of their actions.

Once the incident has been dealt with, move on and **do not** discuss it again. If children persist in stealing seek professional help.

Teenagers

When teenagers are not at school their parents should know or at least have a very good idea, where they are, who they are with and what they are doing. Apply some common sense. If your teenager is out all day with little money and returns home with a new CD, question how they got it.

Honest children can be confronted with whole new peer pressures when they become teenagers. Being supportive and open with your teenagers will help them come to terms with new problems they may be confronted with and make sure they can top up their allowance by doing extra jobs around the house or get a weekend job.

Lying

Not unlike stealing, we don't want to have children who grow up lying to us or anyone else, so we have to encourage our children to tell the truth. The thought of our children growing up and becoming dishonest or deviant is one of a parents' worst nightmares.

Again the best learning tool is a good example but although we may think of ourselves as honest upright citizens and good role models for our children, they just might perceive us differently.

The supper table is the perfect environment to discuss honesty and pose dilemmas for your children, even teenagers enjoy this one. It provides you with the opportunity to hear your children's solutions and impart your own values to a particular problem.

White lies

White lies are part of everyday life. They are not said with the intention to cause malice or harm. They are just sometimes convenient, tactful and polite, but to a young child who has been told always to tell the truth, overhearing them can send mixed messages.

What husband has never told a white lie to his wife's question, "Does this dress make me look fat?" Any with a modicum of self-preservation would answer, "No," even though he may be thinking, "Actually yes, but if I say that we'll never get out tonight."

Who hasn't fibbed when asked about someone's new hairstyle or dress, or cried off an engagement on the telephone feigning illness or your child's upset tummy?

We are all guilty of responding untruthfully to polite pleasantries, for instance: The postman turns up at the door,

Postman: "Good morning, Mrs Smith, how are you?"
Mrs Smith (untruthfully)   "I'm fine thanks, and you?"
Postman: (truthfully)   "Very well, thank you."

But imagine the scenario if we told the absolute truth:

Mrs Smith: "Well, since you've asked, actually I am a woman on the *edge*. My kids don't respect me, my husband doesn't notice me and I've been overlooked for promotion at work. What I need to regain my sanity is a month in The Priory surrounded by fit young men with pert buttocks in white uniforms pandering to my every need!"

Postman: "Could you just sign here for the letter, please Mrs Smith."

"Of course she's twelve."
Naughty, naughty!

In certain situations it is just so much easier and less embarrassing to avoid the truth. If you suspect your child has overheard you telling a little white lie or questioned you over an obvious fib, it is best to be open and honest with them and explain exactly why you did it and apologise.

I have always endorsed honesty in our family, but a few years ago I took my three children to the cinema to see a 12-rated film. When asked by the box-office if my youngest was twelve, I brazenly said, "Yes, of course," to which my youngest piped up, "No I'm not. I'm only 10." Spluttering an embarrassed, ashamed, "Oh, of course you are. How silly of me, I forgot," I hot footed it out of there with two very angry children and one very confused one.

Reasons that children lie

To avoid punishment

Children will lie to avoid punishment and can you blame them? If they know they are going to be shouted at, called names and given a harsh punishment as soon as they own up to a deed, they will deny it.

If, for instance, you find an ornament has been knocked over and broken, jumping up and down screaming, "Right, whoever broke this is in for some serious big trouble and no TV for a month, now who was it?" is hardly going to inspire anyone to run down the stairs admitting, "It was me, it was me." It is going to encourage denial and lying.

However, if you tell your children that if they did break the vase and admit it, you will certainly not be angry. It is then very important not to be angry.

Prevention

Explain to your children that if they break anything or do anything that they think may anger you to own up to it immediately and promise them that you will not be angry and no-one will be punished. Accidents do happen and you would much prefer that they owned up than lied to cover up.

They need to be thanked and praised for telling the truth. Then simply ask your child to tell you how the accident happened and if appropriate help clean it up. Perhaps they can even try and help repair it with you.

While children are young they must be encouraged to tell the truth and praised when they do. But as they get older they must also learn to take responsibility for the consequences of their actions. For example, if your son owns up to breaking your favourite mirror by kicking a football around the sitting room, thank them for telling you but also tell him he should have known better than to play football in the house and he will have to put some of his allowance for the next month towards it.

Explain that 'honesty is the best policy' and however awful they think the consequences of an intentional or unintentional action was, you will be very angry if you find out you have not been told the truth. Emphasise that there is nothing they could do that they can't tell you about.

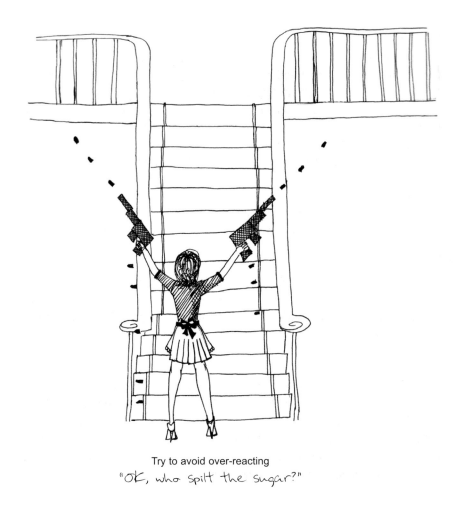

Try to avoid over-reacting

"OK, who spilt the sugar?"

But as well as denying their action they may well lie that someone else did it. This has serious circumstances for an innocent party and must be discouraged.

Children need to understand how lies can devastate people's lives. Tell them that work, relationships and even people's freedom can all be affected by lies and give them an example. Even though it is unlikely that your child's lie is going to put anyone behind bars, they should hear the consequences of where lying can lead.

Children lie to hide inadequacies

Parents' unrealistic expectations of their children's ability can often be the cause of lying and even cheating during tests and exams. For instance, if a father expects his son to get an A grade in his maths exam and he only receives a C, he may well lie about the grade to avoid his fathers displeasure and disappointment, even though the boy knows that his father will eventually find out. Lying simply delays the unpleasantness. Cheating may help him achieve the desired grade but is worthless as it was obtained through dishonesty.

Prevention

Make sure that you don't set such high standards that your children feel under enormous pressure to deliver and may resort to lying if they don't.

Peer pressure

Once children go to school they are desperate to fit in with their new peer group. They may tell untruthful stories to impress classmates, be the centre of attention or because they suffer from low self-esteem and simply don't think anyone would be interested in them if they were just themselves.

Prevention

Improve your child's self-esteem with encouragement and praise.

Once your child starts school and makes a few friends, invite one of them back to your house for tea. It is much easier for children to bond as friends outside the playground away from the scrutiny of the rest of the class. If your children are confident with their friends and realise that they are liked for who they are, they will be less likely to feel they have to impress anyone.

Children lie to get what they want

Children will sometimes lie to get what they want but if challenged will often admit to their inaccuracies. They may say they have finished tidying their room, when actually they haven't, so they can go and play with their friends, but this is a fairly mild lie as a visit to the room will immediately prove otherwise.

They may deny that they've already eaten two chocolate biscuits so they can have some more, but the chocolate rim around their mouth tells another story.

In these type of incidents children are more likely to think they are pushing their luck rather than telling outright lies.

Prevention

If you suspect or can prove that they may be stretching the truth confront them about it. Impose some type of punishment. For instance with the above examples, get them to finish tidying up their room and then they will have to stay in and not see their friends for a day. With the chocolate biscuit incident, there will be no biscuits tomorrow.

Explain that if they had been honest to start with and asked if could see their friends now and promise to finish their room later, you would have probably let them. Or if the chocolate biscuit muncher had owned up immediately, he would have been able to have another biscuit as a reward for being honest.

Lying for attention

Children who may be lacking in parental or social attention may conjure up elaborate stories and tales to attract attention. When they see this ploy works they will continue.

Prevention

Parents pretty quickly cotton-on if their children are telling elaborate stories for attention, so when you have proof, take them aside on a one-to-one basis and tell them that you know the story was an untruth. Avoid asking why they have been telling lies as it will probably prompt another one. After all how many children are going to recognise their problem and say, "Well, Mother it's like this. I'm simply not getting enough of the right type of attention at home, and this seems to be a fairly successful way of attracting it."

Explain to your child that although they may think it is harmless, it is lying and it is not acceptable behaviour.

Start organising a few projects or days out with your children to give them a real story to talk about and then make sure that they do have enough of the right type of attention at home. Reward truthful stories.

Story-telling can also be the a sign of a highly imaginative mind, so stories are OK as long as they are not presented as truth.

School

I can't imagine there is a person reading this who during their school years didn't tell a teacher either:-

a) They'd left their homework at home when in fact it hadn't even been started.
b) They weren't feeling well to get off games.
c) They lied about the real reason that they were late.

Although it would be unrealistic to imagine we are ever going to change school children trying to skive off games, we can explain to children how honesty can minimise being reprimanded by teachers.

School playgrounds are a breeding ground for gossip, tittle-tattle and lies. Whatever age your children are there will always be opportunities for untruths to be told about them or other pupils or teachers.

Prevention
Remaining honest at school can be very difficult for children. Discussing some of the predicaments that may occur is perfect supper conversation for all ages of children. By taking examples and asking their opinions you will be able to hear what their immediate reaction would be and you will be able to offer your opinions and what your family would find acceptable.

For example, if your son was the only person to witness his best friend write 'Miss Spelling is a Bitch,' on the blackboard, Miss Spelling is quite rightly going to ask whoever wrote it or whoever knows who wrote it to tell her, otherwise the entire class will be punished. Your son is thrown into a dilemma. His friend stays silent, the rest of the class know nothing. Should he be honest and tell and lose his friend but save the class from punishment or does he stay quiet? Honesty versus loyalty, what a predicament for a young person.

In my opinion, after the class he should take his friend aside and tell him to go and see the teacher privately and admit what he's done, apologise for being so stupid and get the credit for being honest and not get the entire class into trouble. If he refuses then your son will let the rest of the class know who it was. This threat is likely to work as one child seldom has the loyalty of the entire class and someone else will tell Miss Spelling.

Take another example. On Monday morning, your son suddenly remembers that he hasn't done his maths homework and his teacher, Mr Yorinforitson is going to go beserk. Suggest that rather than wait until the maths lesson starts to admit he doesn't have it (when the teacher can have a real go at him in front of the rest of the class) pre-empt the situation by going immediately to the staff room and asking to see Mr Yorinforitson. Explain how sorry he is but he has not done his homework and guarantee a time by which it will be done. Tell your child to be totally honest as to why it is not done. If he simply forgot, to say he simply forgot, not to make up some elaborate story which the teacher will see straight through. The teacher will be caught off-guard and although he may be annoyed at the work not being done, he will certainly be impressed that the child had been conscientious and honest enough to come and admit his error, tell the truth and offer a solution. Teachers are far more understanding under this type of circumstance and in most cases will thank the child for coming to tell them and accept the situation.

As soon as children realise that honesty can diffuse issues school-life will run more smoothly.

What to do if a child lies

Once you realise or suspect your child has lied, take immediate action.

If you suspect your son has lied (for the first time), take him aside and sit down with him. (Standing up, towering over a child can be far too intimidating.) Ask him to tell you the truth about the particular situation, explain that you will not be angry if he tells you exactly what happened. If he lied, he must own up and tell you, but if he doesn't and you find out he has lied, which you will, you will be very angry. If your children trust you to do as you say, in nearly all cases they will own up. If he is insistent that he did not lie, then you must accept it. If he owns up, explain how hurtful lies can be, give him an example about if someone lied about him, how would he feel. Explain that he must simply never lie, it would upset you so much, no one lie would be worth that.

If you find out that your child has lied again. Adopt a firm tone but **do not** shout and scream, which is only signalling to your child that you have lost control and they need to see that you are very much in control of this situation. Speak to your child on a one-to-one basis with no-one else around. The last thing you need is 'righteous' siblings name calling after the reprimand. Under no circumstance let them make excuses for the lie and do not make an excuse for them. If children are allowed to make excuses or have excuses made for them they will grow up always blaming their lie on someone or something else.

The person who was lied to or lied about must receive an immediate apology. If children make an effort to justify their lie after their apology, stop them immediately and explain there are no excuses for lying. You will probably be able to work out why your child lied as soon as you hear what was said. Explain to your child how they could have avoided lying and if they have a problem where they feel they need to lie to come and talk to you first.

Children must learn that lying is not tolerated.

Unfortunately lying can become a habit very quickly, especially when children realise that they can attract more attention and avoid taking responsibility for their actions.

Try and avoid falling into the trap of overlooking some lies then punishing others. Be consistent. Explain that people who lie are eventually found out because of the inconsistency of their stories. Its easy to tell the truth and recall it but much harder to remember something that was invented.

> When my son was six, he started a new school in a new area and didn't know anyone. He came home a couple of weeks later, bottom lip trembling, and told me that he had been given a black mark. When he said he had no idea what it was for, I said that he must have done something wrong. Black marks aren't just handed out to well-behaved children and he was normally a very good little boy. The next morning I insisted he go to see the teacher and ask what the black mark was for, which he agreed he would do, but that evening he told me that he had forgotten. With the hackles of injustice rising rapidly on my neck, I picked up the telephone and I told my son that I would ring the school and talk to the teacher and ask her because it was obviously worrying him. Before I had time to start dialling, my son 'suddenly remembered' why he was in trouble. He had stuck out his tongue at the teacher behind her back for a dare and another boy had told her. After our little 'honesty' talk he wrote a letter to his teacher apologising for his behaviour.

Teenagers

Privacy

Normally very honest teenagers may lie to protect their privacy. They may not feel ready for a barrage of questions if they have just started a relationship with a member of the opposite sex. This doesn't mean that they will never tell you, it just means that they are not ready to divulge certain information yet.

Teenagers may also lie about where they are going or who they are going with if they think you will disapprove and stop them. Try to get to know their friends. Tell your teenagers to invite a few friends around for pizza and a video. If lines of communication have always been good between you and your children they are more likely to tell you where they are going even if they suspect you will disapprove.

RESPECT

Children simply have to learn how to respect themselves, other people and property.

How to help your child develop self-respect

Children will develop self-respect by receiving love, support, encouragement, praise and discipline. And when they are disciplined it must be made clear that *they* are not bad but it was their behaviour that was bad. When children make mistakes they should be cajoled and encouraged to try again, not belittled by their failed attempt. Accept your child's stage of development and capabilities and never over-face your children with unrealistic expectations. A perception of failure is a quick way for children to lose respect and confidence in themselves.

How to respect your children

It's all very well us moaning that children never show us any respect but we often don't show them the kind of respect we expect from them. I personally don't like to hear parents describe their children as 'brats' and what signal is that sending out if their children overhear? What would those parents think if they heard their children referring to them as 'old farts'? Often name calling is unintentional, parents adopt nicknames for their children which they might think are sweet and funny, but why should 'chubby chops', 'carrot top' or 'freckle face' be any more respectful than children calling their parents, 'baldy', 'fish eyes' or 'thunder thighs'?

If we regularly reprimand and humiliate our children in front of shop loads of customers why should our children worry about screaming for what they want in front of the same people?

The best way for us to show our respect for our children is by being calm, kind and firm in our discipline. Calmness shows we are in control, kindness shows that we care and firmness demonstrates that we know they need to learn. Our children need to feel respected and they will by the way we talk to them, treat them, discipline them and listen to their opinions and wishes. In no way does this mean that we agree with their opinions, give into their every wish or decline to discipline them.

How to get your children to respect you

Your children will immediately start to respect you the minute you start to exercise any discipline on them, as in not letting them get their own way with tantrums, saying, "No," and meaning, "No." Toddlers to four year-olds will push all the buttons to see what kind of power they can exercise within the family and if they do not receive the correct discipline they soon realise that their parents will give in if they moan, resist and irritate them enough. These children develop no respect for their parents and will grow up often treating them with contempt.

How children develop respect for their family

Talk to your children about how to respect other members of the family. Explain how they should always ask if they want to borrow something from a sibling or as they get older even a parent. That they should look after the article whilst it's in their possession and return it. For instance, if your teenage daughter borrows her sister's top she should make sure it is returned clean, even if she has to ask you to wash it.

Respect must also be shown for other family member's feelings and privacy. Explain that if they want to enter a sibling's bedroom they should knock and ask if they can go in and wait for a reply, not just barge in unannounced.

Encourage your children to care about the feelings of other members of the family, if they see a sibling or a parent looking sad or acting in an angry fashion to ask them if they are OK or if there is anything they can do to help.

Respecting other people

The way we treat people is going to be the benchmark for how our children treat people. We should teach our children to respect everyone that they come into contact with regardless of their sex, race, age, religion or profession. They should always show their respect to adults by being polite and courteous in their presence.

Our children will learn to respect other adults by our example. If we bandy around comments like, "Oh let her do it, she's the shop assistant," or "Don't worry, he's just a waiter," or slam the phone down on a telephone sales girl with a, "No I don't want bloody double-glazing," we are unlikely to impress upon our children that these people command our respect.

One place that children absorb the examples we set is in the car and sadly, I am a huge offender here. I have on occasion, shown no respect for speed limits. I have sworn at other drivers on the road and I have voiced loudly my opinion of white van drivers.

However, I always let cars out of side roads, garages, etc. pedestrians across the road and I always thank other drivers who let me out. But I was dismayed to see my daughter who has been driving for a year follow my examples to the letter. She is a courteous driver, occasionally swears at other drivers (usually in white vans) and sometimes drives too fast. Let that be a lesson to us all!

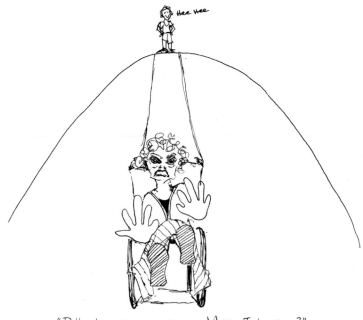

"Billy have you seen Mrs. Johnson?"

Children should to be taught to respect adults.

How to respect their friends

Children often need a few pointers on how to deal with friends. Young children need to understand how to share (see page 24) whether it is their toys, their friends or in emergencies their lunch. When children (of all ages) have fall-outs with their friends, which they regularly do, ask them what happened, what was said and offer some advice on how to sort the problem out. Explain that their friends have feelings and can get as equally angry or hurt and try to get them to empathise with them.

Discourage your children from talking badly or gossiping about friends behind their backs. And explain to them how to be kind, loyal and encouraging. If they notice their friend is unhappy or struggling with a subject discuss ways they could make their friend feel better by finding out what was wrong or suggesting how to get help with their work.

If you notice a friend is dominating your child to the point of bullying or entices your child into behaving badly or being rude, invite some different friends around to your house for your child to mix with. Your children should receive the same respect that they give their friends.

Remind your children always to ask if they would like a drink or a piece of fruit when they are at their friend's house. Explain that if they have a meal they should offer to help lay the table and help clear the plates afterwards. And obviously, they must say thank you when they leave.

How to respect your friends

When you have your friends to visit, your children should always look up from what they are doing, look your friend directly in the eye, smile and say, "Hello," not continue watching glued to the TV and begrudgingly say a sullen, "Hello." As your children get older, encourage them to ask how people are. If your friends are coming round to see you after their holiday, let your children know and suggest it might be polite if they asked how they enjoyed their trip. When appropriate they should help them with their coats and open doors for them. From the age of thirteen, teenagers should have short (or long) conversations with your friends. Teenage boys should shake hands with your male friends.

Occasionally, you are probably going to have friends for supper so the children will be fed first on their own. Explain to young children why you are not eating as a family that particular evening. If they are still up when your friends arrive they must come and say, "Hello," but when you signal it is time to go to bed you would be over-joyed if they went to bed quietly on their own, after saying, "Goodnight," to everyone. Emphasise how grown up your friends will think they are if they do go to bed when asked and if they obey, they will have extra TV time or a treat tomorrow.

Children should accept that when you have friends around and you want to have an adult evening, they are to stay out of the way unless you ask them otherwise.

Respecting property

Again it is by example. If we let our children jump and walk all over armchairs and sofas at home, they will think it is perfectly acceptable behaviour to do exactly the same in someone else's home. Equally in your own home, stop your children from putting their feet up on tables and make sure their shoes are off if they put their feet up on sofas. I know when they are little it doesn't seem too harmful but it'll drive you crazy when suddenly they're teenagers with their size 10's resting on your coffee table.

If your children see you kicking their toys to one side when they're under your feet, they will think this is an entirely acceptable way to treat their own or someone else's belongings. Ideally every day, but let's be realistic here, once a week, ask your child to help you pick up all their toys and put them neatly away or in little displays around their room. Try and mend any broken toys and wipe clean any toys that are filthy. All these small amounts of effort will show your child how to respect their things and will extend to respecting other people's belongings as well.

Once children have started nursery school or as soon as they can hold a pencil, always have plain paper for them to draw on and stop them drawing in story books, whatever condition they may be in. The next book they ruin could be a first edition Harry Potter.

Encourage, in fact, insist that your children always put their empty carton of drink or an apple core in the bin whether at home or out. Again, if they shown from a very early age and praised when they do it they will happily oblige when they remember. Of course, when they become teenagers, they may have to be reminded all over again.

Contributing to household work

Children will also learn to respect furnishings and personal property if they have to help look after them. Just because we are the parents and providers for our children, there is no reason why our children cannot start helping us around the house. The younger they start, the more natural it will be for them to help for when they are older and can tackle real jobs.

Whatever job you ask them to do, starting with simple jobs, show them how to do it first. If it's dusting for example, show them how to pick up any objects and dust under them, not around them (and yes, it is amazing the amount of people who don't know that). However, don't expect them to dust around any precious objects when they are very young for obvious reasons.

And don't blow it by giving them inappropriate, long or to difficult tasks that will make them lose interest immediately. You will be surprised at how willing young children are to help around the house, and if they have to do something every day or three times a week, they will grow up expecting to help and why shouldn't they, it's their family home not a hotel.

Of course, suddenly asking a thirteen year old to start hoovering when they've never lifted a finger to help, is likely to get you a confused. "Get serious wot's an' oover?" However, it's never too late to learn. Show them how to do a certain chore and let them get on with it, but it would be unwise to overwhelm them immediately. So for instance, if you are hoovering, just ask them to hoover the sitting room and hall, not the entire house or flat.

it is very important that whatever job they do, however small, it is done well. And do not be afraid to make them do it again, if it is not done properly. Again this is a great lesson for when they're at school or in the work place, they are never to young to learn that if they are going to do a job they must do it to the best of their ability.

If on some days they are a bit reluctant to do anything don't bribe them into doing work with the offer of a reward, but occasionally, treat them to a little surprise, as a thank you.

Keeping their rooms tidy

I would love to be able to give you infallible advice about how to get your children to keep their rooms tidy, but I can't. From my experience it appears to be endemic in all children, not just mine.

Things children never say:

"Tidy my room mum? Why of course I'll do it straight away."

I can't imagine any child replying to the age old request, "Will you please go and tidy your room," with, "Why of course, Mum, that's a great idea, I'll go and do it straight away." I suspect it will always be a case of bribery. Personally, I never minded seeing my son's carpet covered in a battle scene with the entire cast of Star Wars versus the Ninja Turtles. At least it showed he was using his imagination. I also used to enjoy the entire space used up by his Scaletrix so I could show him my imagination by banking up the corners of the track with several large books and driving the cars at such a speed that they would shoot off the steep corner onto the window-sill (it clearly doesn't take much to amuse me.)

People who want orderly houses and lives don't have children, they have shoe cupboards!

If you ask children under the age of ten to clear up their room, as soon as they start, they will become engrossed with some toy or other and the room may end up worse than when they started. The only way is to help them. Suggest they pick up their clothes while you pick up their toys.

When they get to an age where they no longer play with toys, once a week ask them to have a quick tidy around their room to help out, make sure they have a waste bin in their room and plenty of hangers. If your children have enough hanging space in their cupboard, show them how to use a hanger (you think I jest?) It's much easier to hang up shirts, T-shirts and jumpers than trying to fold them. Give your children a dirty-washing basket or bag and let them know that only clothes in the basket get washed. Help them organise their room to try to help them to keep it tidier. Insist they take out the glasses and mugs growing mould that Alexander Fleming would have been proud of.

As they become teenagers they may well want to get shot of the Superman or Winnie the Pooh duvet and matching pillowcase set. If you help them to turn their bedroom into a more grown-up room (but girls will never cull the soft toy collection), you may find that they will take more of a pride in it, especially if it is somewhere they can take their friends. Put the occasional vase of flowers in your daughters room.

How to respect your teenagers

Teenagers are half adult and half child and the needs of both must be met. When children become teenagers they enter another development stage of battling for their independence. And in a way it is no different to the terrible twos, your children still need your love, kindness, support, guidance, patience and good example.

Teenagers have to cope with a minefield of changes; feelings, hormones, peer pressure, exams and new relationships can each make them feel frustrated, moody and unreasonable. Try and empathise with their feelings, imagine PMT with *SERIOUS ATTITUDE*. You see, suddenly *we know* how they're feeling.

The first noticeable difference when they reach this age is their need for privacy which you must always respect. Always knock on their bedroom door and ask if you can go in, don't just knock and enter. If they spend too long in the bathroom, rather than shout and lecture them, just ask if they could please hurry up. Later, discuss a way around the bathroom scenario. Perhaps you could allocate a time for them when they could linger in the bathroom. If girls want to do their hair and make up in the bathroom because the light is better, treat them to an electric make-up mirror for their bedroom.

Parents have their own privacy issues and there are certainly areas of adult life which should not involve children, even when they become teenagers. Teenagers must respect your privacy as you respect theirs. This is a lesson best demonstrated by example.

But not unlike us, teenagers respond badly to being shouted at or lectured. Another characteristic of teenagers is that they can appear unreasonable, frustrating and generally difficult. Always go for the sit down, eye-to-eye chat together to try to resolve any issues. Allow them to speak without interrupting and listen to them. You may not agree or wish to comply with their suggestions but they are of an age you must listen and discuss, not simply brush them aside.

The best way to help support your children through adolescence is to be involved in what's happening in their lives and talk to them on a daily basis.

Once again, the supper table is a good time to talk to them about going out in the evenings and to discuss how to handle peer pressure in regard to taking drugs, drinking, girl and boyfriends etc. If there are much younger siblings present find somewhere else to have your chat. Never tease teenagers about relationships, just ask straightforward questions if you want to know anything about them. Do not let siblings tease about relationships either. Teenagers are trying to assert themselves as adults and wish to be treated as such to a certain degree. Any type of teasing is likely to prevent them telling you anything for the foreseeable few years. Underneath their adult bravado, teenagers are in fact very vulnerable. Apart from the physical affection they may be getting elsewhere, your teenagers still need physical affection from you. Give them an assuring hug or sit and watch TV with your arm around them or give them a shoulder massage while you talk to them.

We've all been fashion victims at one time or other.

Clothes

We are all guilty at some stage of wearing clothes that we probably shouldn't (check your old photos) and when teenagers start to choose their own clothes, they may not be exactly what we would choose for them. Whether they are wearing something to be fashionable, make a statement or be individual, think positively before you pass comment.

Try to avoid criticising, so rather than being derogatory, "What on earth are you wearing, those jeans look awful?" say something positive, such as, "I preferred those trousers you were wearing the other day, you looked great in them."

Teenagers are full of insecurities and anxieties especially about their body shape and looks, so help to build their confidence. Everyone has good points so for instance, when they bemoan the fact that they've got a fat waist, tell them not to worry because they've got drop-dead gorgeous legs.

If girls are wearing too much make-up avoid snapping, "You're not going out with all that muck on your face," kindly suggest that they really don't need that much make-up and with their looks a more natural style would be more attractive. Even offer to treat your daughter to a make-up lesson at a local department store or beauty salon so she can see what suits her. Prime the salon first that you want a natural look.

Health

Thanks to permanent media exposure of supposedly idealised body shapes of women and men, nearly all teenage girls and some boys are concerned about their weight. Explain to them that it is perfectly normal to gain some weight and experience normal physical changes during adolescence. Suggest a healthy diet and exercise programme for them to follow and help them achieve it by having healthy snacks and plenty of fruit in the home. Unhealthy weight goals for models, actresses and celebrities is also a good topic to talk about at supper.

Compliment your children on their shape and never, ever comment that they are overweight or fat. That is a sure way to start eating problems. If you feel your children are overweight make sure they have a healthy calorie-controlled supper and don't keep any high-fat, high-sugar snacks in the house, they will appreciate your support and understand. Suggest you all join a local fitness centre or take up jogging.

Drinking

Once your teenagers are about fourteen if you are out to dinner ask them if they would like a little wine mixed with water to drink. The French have always brought their children up this way and they seem to have avoided the culture of binge-drinking. What it does do is show your respect for your teenager in that you judge they are grown up enough to cope with it. Invariably they won't even like the taste and will stick with water or juice. But if teenagers are offered alcohol by their parents, the need to go and try it behind their backs loses its appeal.

Teenage problems

Drugs, unwanted pregnancies, teenage depression and eating disorders are all foreseeable problems which concern (terrify) all parents.
Explain to your teenagers that there is no subject, however awful, unlawful or shameful that cannot be discussed with you. There is no problem that is so great that you cannot work something out together. If you have all regularly

talked together, by the time your children are teenagers they will know exactly how you feel about teenage sex, pregnancies, drugs and diets. Spending time together at regular family meals will make the job of identifying any problems a little easier. If you are a close family, you will soon notice any change in your child's behaviour. As soon as you do, try and talk privately to your child about your concerns. If they are not forthcoming, discuss the problem with their teacher and if it continues seek professional help.

How to get your teenager's respect

Avoid head to head arguments. All they will achieve is bad feeling on both sides. Arguments often end up with unnecessary name calling and accusations that both parties will later regret. Keep calm, don't swear, don't bring up past problems, respect and listen to what your child has to say. While your child is talking resist the temptation to interrupt, accuse or judge. Listen properly and respond.

When you raise an issue with them just stick to one thing at a time. If the immediate problem is poor results in recent school exams, discuss that and ways to solve it, don't drag in other issues....your room is always untidy....you don't help enough around the house. And avoid trying to get too personal, *you're* this and *you're* that is not treating your children with the respect they deserve and you can hardly blame them for starting to reply, "Yea well *you're*...." Just as with small children it is necessary to be clear it is not the child who displeases but their behaviour/friends/attitude you are not keen on.

Continually telling your teenager how awful they are is likely to become a self-fulfilling prophecy for them. However, if you tell them they are responsible and that you trust them, they are far less likely to let you down. Once they start going out with their friends, let them know what your expectations of them are, what sort of an allowance they can have.

Always try and set a good example. After all, if your children see you smoking, the worse for wear from drink, or permanently on some sort of diet, they are going to think it is OK for them to do the same.

Teenagers will rebel against lecturing and preaching. Talk to them adult to adult. Even as adults they must realise that there are still rules and let them know what the consequences will be if the rules are broken.

HOW TO BEHAVE IN PUBLIC

Restaurants

Nothing can ruin a good restaurant meal quicker than badly behaved children. If parents have not taught their children table manners at home, then why do they inflict them on the defenceless public who have decided to spend their hard earned cash on a meal out?

"Child restraint for table 9!"

What makes some parents think that their children are going to sit still for an hour around a dining table, when they have never sat still at home longer then ten minutes, and that was with the TV on? It is especially unfair on the children who have no idea how to behave in any other way. Think of it from their point of view. They are told that they are going to a restaurant with their parent(s) for a treat, and they are berated the entire time they are there for behaving they way they are allowed to at home. Mixed messages are very confusing for children.

And however harmless parents may think it is for their children to be allowed to run around the restaurant, it is highly annoying for the staff, inconsiderate to other diners and dangerous to the children in case they have a hot meal or a tray of drinks spilt on them. Parents must be considerate and conscientious.

As your children gradually learn how to eat correctly at home, (Table manners, page 69) you can start taking them to restaurants. But take it slowly. Do not for instance, take your youngsters to a Michelin three star on their first outing. Start with casual, child-friendly places like Pizza restaurants or cafes, and as you all gain confidence, gradually move on to more formal restaurants, and choose one near home in case of tantrums, (theirs or yours).

Eventually when your children do know how to behave at a table, a trip to an adult restaurant will be a very exciting treat for them. Children love to do what adults do, especially with their parents. Let them know that it is a real restaurant, that there will be very few other children, but it is a special treat because they do know how to behave amongst adults. French, Italian or Spanish restaurants are a good choice as the staff are generally far more family oriented and tolerant of children.

However, leaving nothing to chance, it is advisable before you get to the restaurant, to run through what is expected of them and what they must try to remember:-

- That it is adults' time, and very best table manners would be appreciated.
- Try and keep voices down
- Decide who is going to sit where and opposite whom before you go in, and reiterate that there will be no change of seating plan once in the restaurant.
- To say, "Good evening," to the waiter/waitress, looking them in the eye.
- To thank the person who takes their coat.
- Sit down in the bar area or at the table without any fuss.
- Try not to fiddle with their knife and fork, and not to play with the salt, pepper or sugar.
- Keep elbows off the table.
- Turn all mobile phones off and no texting at the table.
- No arguing.
- To remember to say, "Please," and "Thank you."

Depending on the restaurant children will either put their own napkin on their laps or the waiter will. Small children can still have their napkin tucked into their collar to save their clothes. If you know fizzy drinks make your children hyper, give them water or orange juice. Sit siblings that are likely to antagonise each other as far apart as possible and if you have a child that is still struggling with a knife and fork, seat them next to yourself or your partner, so you can help them.

When you have helped your children decide what they are going to eat, let them order for themselves, even if it is in French, let them repeat it after you. You'll be amazed at how patient waiters(esp. French, Italian and Spanish) are with children. Make sure the children look at the waiter while they are ordering, followed by, "Please."

Show them how to break off a piece of their bread roll at a time, then butter and eat it, before breaking off another. And however tempting it is, don't let them fill up on too much bread, as it will probably only annoy you if they cannot eat their meal.

If your children are still young help them with the menu and let them order something you know they like. As they get older, encourage them to try new dishes, and if they choose something which requires a special way of eating, i.e. mussels, show them how to eat them. Also be prepared for them to dislike certain things, so either suggest ordering it yourself and sharing it or don't get upset if they don't like it. If there is nothing except chips that they like on the menu, then just let them have chips. It's far more important that you all enjoy the evening than get stressed out about its nutritious content. Don't be afraid to ask for small portions, which is far less overwhelming for children, although you'll probably still pay the same.

When the food arrives, they must thank the waiter, then wait until everyone has been served their food before they start. However, if there is a bit of a wait for one dish, tell the others to start.

Stay calm, even if the odd accident happens, such as a water glass getting knocked over or a potato flying onto the floor. The more relaxed you are, the more relaxed your children will be.

Make the evening treat really enjoyable for them, talk to them about holidays, funny stories, anything to keep the evening flowing. If there is more than one child, make sure they all have plenty of opportunity to join in with all the conversations.

Finally, get the children to thank the waiters and say goodnight. In all likelihood, if they have been well-behaved, the waiter will comment upon it, reinforcing their sense of pride, *and yours!*

After you have left, if they all behaved well, tell them how proud you are of them, ask them if they enjoyed the evening and would they like to do it again. If there were a few minor hiccups there's no point saying you've never been so embarrassed in all your life, (because it's probably untrue), but how pleased you were the way they were polite to the waiter or tried a new dish.

Things that can go wrong

Problem
Children start arguing with each other.
Solution
Very quietly, but very firmly tell them to stop and engage them in a different topic.

Problem
Crying because they have burnt their tongue.
Solution
Give them a glass of water, sympathise, but ask them to cry quietly. (It works!) Otherwise take them out of the restaurant until they stop.

Problem
A child throws a tantrum.
Solution
Quickly remove the child from the table and take them out of the earshot of other diners or outside if necessary, and stay with them until it is over, then calmly explain that behaviour like that is not acceptable at the table. When they are quiet take them back to the table and immediately start talking about something else. Do not refer to the episode again. Every restaurateur I have spoken to has asked me to add that if your child is crying, take them out of the restaurant.

Problem
They are too loud.
Solution
Children are not used to speaking quietly at home, so they just need reminding that it is adult time and to keep their voices down.

Problem
A fit of the giggles.
Solution
Very few people are offended by laughter, just try and keep the volume down.

Problem
A child keeps getting up from the table.
Solution
Sit them next to you and explain they are not to get down again. Then talk to them about something they are interested in to keep their attention. If they try to get down again, hold their arm firmly to prevent them.

Problem
A child becomes very sleepy.
Solution
If you have not finished your meal, tell them to close their eyes and let them sleep in a sitting position, not with their head on the table. If they are just toddlers let them sit next to you with their head resting in your lap. They may otherwise fall off the chair.

Problem
A child becomes very upset, or ill.
Solution
Occasionally, you will just have to cut your losses and take them home.

Trains and buses

We've all experienced on the tube or train, a group of teenagers sitting opposite each other, feet up on the seats, surrounded by their empty crisp packets and fizzy drink cans, personal stereos cranked up so loud that people in the next town can hear them and using the 'f' word as though their life depended on it.

Do we want our children to be like that when they grow up? I don't think so. So, just like everything else, we must start showing our children how to behave on public transport from an early age.

When queuing to get on a bus or train, always wait to let the people get off before you get on, and explain to your child what you are doing and why. If the bus or train is crowded and you have to squeeze past, prompt your child to say, "Excuse me, please, and thank you," as you try and find a seat. If you happen to knock into someone, then apologise.

When the ticket collector or conductor comes around, let your child show them the tickets and remind them to look into their face and say, "Good morning," or, "Hello," and smile. If you add, "Hello, how are you today?" your child will see that you are making an effort to be polite. Have you ever watched train and bus conductors collecting tickets? Most people don't even look up, and if they do they are expressionless, so how hard is a smile and a simple pleasantry, especially if brightens up someone's day? Unfortunately, you may not always receive the reaction you were expecting, however cheerful you are, but then there are some people a lottery win wouldn't cheer up. But children should be aware of all human emotions, so let your child know in a confidential whisper, "What a misery, I wonder what he was so grumpy about?"

When your children are about four-years-old, if you are seated on the tube, train or bus when it is full, explain to your child that you would like them to ask an adult if they would like their seat and explain why. You can attract the person's attention then prompt your child to ask, do not do it for them. Boys *and* girls can do this, and they don't have to give up their seat just to some very elderly person, someone in their 20's who's been working all day, would equally appreciate it. By making your child ask, the recipient will thank the child personally. Children love attention, but there are right ways and wrong ways of getting it. And a knowing smile from the recipient in your direction, saying, 'At last a parent who knows how to bring up her children,' won't go down so badly either.

Toddlers and young children invariably want to get up and run around or play on public transport, which can be dangerous and highly annoying for other travellers. They should sit or stand next to you. Encourage them to remain seated by getting them to point things out from the window and have a small book or toy handy in your pocket to amuse them. Keep a few finger puppets in every bag you have so that you always have them on hand to entertain your youngsters. Sometimes, however, they will be over-tired or hungry and restless but resist the urge to let them start walking or playing around. Try and distract them with a little story, play, 'I Spy' or ask them to see how many people are wearing the colour red? Use your imagination, keep calm and keep them seated or next to you.

If you are eating or drinking in transit, when you arrive at your destination find a bin and dispose of your litter or take it with you and explain to your child what you are doing. If you see used coffee cups and wrappers left on seats, point it out to your children and say how selfish it was of someone to leave their rubbish behind, which looks untidy and someone else will have to remove. If it's next to you, just dump it yourself.

By registering your disapproval or approval at different situations, your children will learn to know what is acceptable and what is not. Obviously, if you leave a chocolate wrapper and empty drinks bottle on the seat when you go, you are teaching your child that this sort of behaviour is acceptable. Remember, your children will learn just as much from the way they see you behave as to what you say.

Don't let it be your child

As they get older, make sure your children put their feet on the floor and never on the seats, and always make sure they bin their rubbish or take it with them and dispose of it afterwards.

When your children are old enough to first start travelling on their own, remind them that there will be other members of the public with them and to remember:

• be courteous to ticket collectors and other travellers

• do not push past people

- no feet on the seats
- give up their seat to an adult
- keep voices down
- bin their litter
- no swearing if they can be overheard
- to give a hand if they see someone struggling to get a pushchair or suitcase onto the train
- if there has been a group of them with just a few other people in a carriage and suspect they have made too much noise, to simply say, "Sorry about the noise," as they leave
- keep incoming mobile calls to a minimum
- make outgoing calls in uncrowded passageways or between carriages

Your reaction at reading this will probably be "GET REAL," but if you have already taught your child how to behave on transport, you will also probably know their weakness, i.e. having their personal stereo too loud, too many phone calls; so you only have to mention what is relevant. And say it in a very casual, "Bye, have a good time, and oh, by the way, don't forget to keep the stereo down…" or, "I know I don't have to tell you but no feet on the seats……Enjoy yourself."

However, if you suspect they contravene all of the above, a quick reminder of feet, swearing, litter and a general awareness that there are other people travelling will do. But again, not in a nagging way, give them the benefit of the doubt that they are going to behave well. Trust them and tell them that you trust them. So something like, "I know you won't let me or yourself down darling, but remember no feet on the seats, no litter and no swearing, there may be people just like me in your carriage. Have a wonderful time. Bye."

Cars

Children arguing, fighting and crying in the back of a car can be hazardous for the driver who is trying to concentrate on the road. It shouldn't have to be said but always strap your child into the back of the car. I often see young children standing up between the two front seats. If the driver has to stop suddenly, the child is liable to serious injury.

Toddlers

With very young children tie a favourite toy to the door side of baby chairs or bumper seats with a piece of ribbon or cord just short enough that a sibling cannot snatch it away, it also prevents tears as it cannot fall on the floor. If there is arguing or tears in the back of the car, ask them to, "Be quiet," in a very firm voice. If they continue, pull the car over to park in a safe place (obviously this is not always possible,) get out, go round to the passenger side back door and open it and let them know in a very firm voice just how angry you are and how their noise is putting everyone in danger. Whether they understand or not, the tone of your voice should be enough to frighten them into silence. Sometimes they need to see and hear how angry you are with them.

> I remember when my daughter was about four and my son about two, they were winding each other up in the back of the car, poking each other until one was crying. I asked them to stop on more than one occasion and finally as the traffic slowed down I turned around to be a bit firmer, then CRUNCH, metal on metal, I back-ended the car in front. Why the woman in front of me decided to stop and let someone cross the road is anyone's guess. Anyway, I got out, we swapped insurance details and I got back in the car and guess what, the children were silent. I drove home without saying a word to them. Sometimes silence is more powerful than words.

School age children

There can still be squabbles and fights whatever their ages. Demand they stop arguing in a very firm voice, if they don't, find somewhere to pull off the road. Turn around and tell them you will just wait by the side of the road until they can guarantee they will stop as you are not prepared to drive on and risk an accident with the disturbance in the back. Restrict the use of game boys at home, so they can play with them in the car. Personal stereos are also great for keeping the children from squabbling.

Airports and aeroplanes

Not unlike ourselves, our children will probably be feeling extremely excited at the prospect of their impending holiday, so we must expect their behaviour to be more exuberant than normal and make allowance for it. With so many things to touch and see and all the hanging around, airports are a testing time for parents and children. However, we don't want them to behave in such a way that we begin our holiday in need of dire psychological help.

How to make your travelling less painful

The night before you go and again on the way to the airport, have a team talk. Explain to your children that you realise they will be excited, nonetheless they will be in a public place and you would like them to be on best behaviour, no running around, no climbing on furniture, no arguments and no loud voices. Each child will be given a small amount of money to buy something at the airport either a toy or a book. They should also pack a book, game boy, personal stereo or something to keep them occupied. It's a good idea if they each pack a small bottle of water or juice. Tell them if you are going to eat anything at the airport or wait until you get on the plane, so there are no arguments once there. Explain that there will probably be a queue before going through to 'Departures' and they will just wait quietly with you. Ask if they have any questions, is there any part of what has been said that they do not understand.

Checking-in

As soon as you arrive at the airport, there is an overriding temptation for your children to push a baggage trolley or sit on one and be pushed. It's fun, it's something you can't do at home and there's (sometimes) plenty of space to do it. But, at the risk of sounding like a complete misery, it can be very dangerous if children are allowed to push other children. Trolleys at most airports actually carry a small sign prohibiting children sitting on them. So if you allow your children to sit on the trolley just make sure there is an adult pushing them.

At the check-in desk keep your children with you. They should not climb on the bag conveyor belt next to the desk and they should not be allowed to fiddle with the customer care barriers or run around.

Toddlers

Toddlers seldom want to stay in their pushchair, so crouch down and try and keeping them there by reading or telling them a story. Show them a brochure of where you are going (if you have one) and get them to point particular items in the pictures, such as beach umbrellas, boats, bicycles. Always keep a couple of finger puppets in your bag for travel and play peek-a-boo with them. If they start getting fidgety take them out of their pushchair, but put reins on them so they cannot wander off. If they make a fuss about having reins on, give them the choice, reins or pushchair and let them decide. Toddlers will need help with escalators so make sure you don't have too much hand baggage.

School-age children

Any type of travelling is the perfect opportunity to let your children use their game boys or other hand-held games and they will be even more appreciative if they do not use them every day. Keep your children with you and don't let them run around the airport where they can get hurt, run into someone else or get lost.

The departure lounge

Toddlers

Don't let them run around on their own or climb on furniture. All toddlers are inclined to wander off, so keep them in reins to avoid them getting lost. The last thing you want is the stress of a lost child before your holiday.

If your toddler is going to have to sit still on a plane, then walk them around the airport, there's always plenty of things you can show them. You can hardly expect them to sit still in the departure lounge and then sit still on the plane. Some airports even have indoor or outdoor viewing areas to watch planes take-off and land.

If you can find the time (you wish), ring the airport before you leave home to find out what facilities they have for young children.

Remember to avoid giving them fizzy drinks and confectionery as they will get an immediate sugar rush and will find it especially difficult to sit still and behave. If you give them a brown bread sandwich as you get on board the carbohydrates are likely to make them a bit sleepy.

School-age children

Let them spend their 'bribe' money at one of the shops and then they can sit quietly and play with whatever they bought. Basically children of this age should not be loud or run around. If they have to move past other passengers sitting down to get to you they say, "Excuse-me, please." When you queue to get through the gate, they wait with you and don't run around or climb on furniture.

On the aeroplane

Before you get on the plane, decide who is going to sit where and next to whom, so there is no arguing in the confined space of the cabin. Remind your children to look at the steward or stewardess, smile and say, "Hello," "Good morning," etc, as you file onto the plane. Get your children seated before you put your hand-luggage in the overhead storage.

If your children are given junior activity packs, ask them to look up to the stewardess and say, "Thank you." Take some small cartons of juice or small bottles of water with you to avoid waiting for the drinks trolley to come around. Cartons are less likely to get knocked over and leak as much. Teach your child not to squeeze cartons so prevent the straw becoming a fountain.

The majority of airlines will provide children's meals if they are ordered at the time of booking, so rather than being offered breast of chicken in some unrecognisable congealed sauce, they can have child-friendly foods, such as baked beans and sausages. It's also a good idea to order a couple of fruit plates at the same time that the whole family can share. But they must be pre-ordered. Otherwise take some fruit on board with you. If your child is a fussy eater take a favourite sandwich.

If your children wish to request something from the drinks trolley, remind them to ask politely for it, looking into the face of the steward or stewardess and then thanking them.

Too many children and adults when asked if they would like a drink, order one without even lifting their heads.

Be aware that your children do not swing their legs and kick the back of the seat in front of them, or stand on their seats and stare or make faces at the person behind them. However endearing you may think this is, the passenger behind probably won't. Explain that they should talk in low voices so not to disturb fellow passengers.

On long haul flights, it is quite acceptable to walk up and down the aisles with young children to stretch their legs, but never let them go on their own. With the new threat of DVT show all the family how to do some leg and arm exercises (see the in-flight magazine), but without kicking the seat infront.

Undoubtedly you will have to visit the toilet while on board. There is a sign asking passengers to wipe down the basin and leave it clean for the next person. As you will be accompanying young children, explain *why* you are wiping the basin and leaving it looking clean, they can even help. When your school-age children go, just gently remind them what the sign says and what to do. I know it sounds that we are always on at these children but gentle reminders are not nagging. Eventually one day, they will do all these things we tell them automatically. It simply makes them more considerate people.

> My crowning moment as a mother came when my son was nine and we were on a flight to Disneyworld with friends and their children.

> As we were late checking-in, our families did not get to sit together and my son sat next to his friend some way from us. Towards the end of the flight I went to see them and an air-hostess asked me if Sam was my child. Thinking the worst, I hesitantly admitted he was, to be told by a smiling hostess that he was by far the most polite child she had ever encountered on a flight. She sang his praises for a good few minutes and finished with, "I'd like to marry him when he's older." The fact that his manners were being extolled by an extremely attractive, shapely blonde was not lost on Sam.

The baggage hall

Just when everyone is tired and bored we have to confront the misery of the baggage hall. If waiting wasn't bad enough we have to put up with insufficient toilets and inadequate seating. Keep a few unwritten postcards to hand to let your children write whilst they are waiting and even have a throw-away camera ready for them to amuse themselves. However, do not let your children play near or touch the baggage carousel. Why, when there are often great big signs saying, 'DANGER - KEEP CHILDREN AWAY FROM THE BAGGAGE CAROUSEL' or 'KEEP YOUNG CHILDREN BEHIND THE YELLOW LINE' do parents blatantly

THE THINKER

"But he likes climbing"
Taken from the
'Lame excuses 'Я' us'
school of parenting.

DO NOT TOUCH

ignore them? Do they think that their children are immune to losing a finger or getting their clothing caught and being dragged screaming along the floor?

Small children can easily get hurt just standing around with their parents in the bustling confusion of other travellers reclaiming their luggage.

If there are two adults, or one adult and an older child, one of them should go and sit (if possible) with the young children away from the carousel and wait, whilst the other adult collects the bags. If you are on your own, tell your child to hold on to the trolley and look after it, then when you see your bags arriving on the carousel, tell your child to help by holding onto the trolley whilst you fetch them. Tell them it is very important that no-one takes the trolley and they are in charge. This will give them a mission which they will enjoy.

Public places

When you are out, for instance, in the park, do not allow your child to climb or jump on the park benches or the flower beds. They are there for the use and pleasure of the public, not for the sole amusement of your child. And despite how harmless you think your child is, do not ignore signs such as, 'Please keep off the grass', or 'Do not feed the ducks'. So explain to your child what the signs mean and depending on their age, why you or they, think the signs are there and why they should be obeyed.

Make sure litter is put in the litterbins, and if you cannot find one, take your litter home with you.

Don't let your children shout and scream and generally make a nuisance of themselves. Yes, this does sound obvious, but parents can become oblivious to their children kicking a ball or throwing a Frisbee around too close to other people and shouting at each other.

- Obey signs

- Don't shout

- Don't stand or play on benches, statues etc

- Be considerate to others members of the public

- Respect public property

- Put litter in bins or take it home

- Don't eat in the street

Teenagers

- Not to swear where they can be overheard

- If they are walking on pavements or paths with friends, move to single file to let oncomers pass. If they are on a pavement, move to the outside and let oncomers pass on the inside.

Shops

Let's face it shopping with young children can be a nightmare. In fact shopping with *men* can be a nightmare as they all have an interest span that lasts about 10 minutes. Children are not naughty for the sake of being naughty in shops. They are fascinated by the contents and then they become bored stiff. They watch you pick up and examine things and then put them back and seemingly can't understand why they cannot do the same. In clothes shops, young children love to run around under the hanging clothes, not because they think it is going to wind you up but because it's more fun than doing nothing.

If at all possible try and organise someone to look after your child while you go alone, even offer to do a friend's shopping if she takes your child and offer to do the same for her. But if you have to take young children explain to them eye-to-eye exactly what shops you are going into and how you expect them to behave. It's worth investing in a comic and the promise of a reward if they will sit and read while you are trying on an outfit. Shopping is also a good time to let young children listen to a favourite story on a personal CD player. Slightly older children can play on their Gameboy or listen to their personal stereos. Insist children say, "Thank you," and "Goodbye," to shop assistants.

Supermarkets

Try and start buying many of your household goods on-line and have them delivered, (if you are lucky enough to live within their delivery area.) Your first on-line shopping list may take some time and you may think it would have been quicker to go and get it yourself. But many of these 'shopping lists' are kept in the supermarket's on-line memory, so products you usually buy every week will automatically appear and you only have to tick if you want them, saving ages searching for each item. Buying on-line will cut down the amount of time you have to spend (if any) in the supermarket. It also avoids your children grabbing everything off the shelf that takes their fancy.

If you prefer to choose your own meat, fish, fresh fruit and vegetables then just shop for those products which will not take too long. Depending where you live try and buy the fresh produce from local suppliers which is far more personal, more interesting for your children and will help keep these individual shops in business.

If you do have to visit the supermarket, on the way there, tell your children how you are going to need their help. Children love to be given responsibility, so to get their full commitment, the first time, try a little reverse psychology.
For example in the car:

Parent: "I'm going to need some help in the supermarket today," (then as though thinking aloud) "But it really is a job for an older child."

This will probably prompt your child to say, "I can do it."

Otherwise say, "Although you are only three, I think you are clever enough to try, would you like to help me?"

Invariably a child will say, "Yes." And now they have a mission they will be much more focused and less likely to play around. Children genuinely like to be given responsibility and help their parents.

Ideas for children to help in supermarkets:

Hand them fruit or vegetables to put in the bag. Show them what you look for in a good apple and show them how to avoid a bruised one. Show them how to choose ripe tomatoes. Ask them to count them out or do it with them. As they get a little older let them bag up the fruit and vegetables on their own. Point out and show them different fruits such as lychee or star fruit and ask if they would like to try one at home. Getting your children to take an active interest in healthy foods is another step forward to getting them to eat healthy foods.

If the supermarket has fruit and veg scales, show your child how to weigh the items. Your child may have to stand in the trolley to reach them.

Once children are about six, show them how you check for a ripe (boxed) camembert by taking the lid off and pressing with your thumb in the middle, over the paper, to see how squashy (ripe) it is.

Ask them what other members of the family like to eat, which cereals, fruit etc. Where possible ask them to take the item off the shelves and put it in the trolley.

At the checkout ask your child to say, "Hello," "Thank you," and "Goodbye," to the checkout girl. If they are old enough, they can help bag up, explain how you would like fruit and veg in one bag, dairy in another and pass them the items accordingly.

Although these suggestions will make the shopping take longer it will reduce the risk of a nervous breakdown.

Cinemas and Theatres
As in other public places children should keep their voices down in public areas. Decide before you go into the auditorium who is going to sit next to who. Once inside either the cinema or theatre if you have to squeeze past people already seated, remind your children to say, "Excuse-me please, thank you." When you reach your seats sit down quickly and quietly. Do not let them put their feet up on the seats in front or kick the seat in front. Once the film has started they should remain quiet and still. There's nothing worse than trying to watch a movie with some child leaping up and down in front of you. If you know your child cannot keep still, either sit right at the back or wait till the film is out on video.

If your children are going to have a packet of sweets, before the film starts tell them to try and be as quiet as possible when they open them and keep the rustling to a minimum. Ask them to turn mobile phones off and remind them not to text.

Waiting rooms – dentist's, doctor's....
Many waiting rooms provide a children's box of toys and books, so there is

something to occupy them. But again just ask them to keep their voices down and do not let them run around. If the waiting room is full and your son is taking up a seat, tell him to ask an adult if they would like it and put your child on your lap or let him stand next to you. Do not let your children climb on the furniture.

Church

Explain before you enter the church that they must only talk in whispers until the service begins and sit quietly with you, there will be no running around. When the minister/priest is addressing the congregation they must sit still and try and listen.

Simple (but extremely important) courtesies

All the following courtesies are easily taught by explanation, example and reminders. They will be highly appreciated by the recipient.

Please and Thank You

There is simply no substitute for these words and no excuse why children or anyone else should not use them each and every time they are appropriate.

It seems so obvious it should not even have to be written about. But how many times have we heard a child asking for something and the mother asks, "What's the magic word?" Spookily, "Now!" seems to be the most popular response. But seemingly more and more children even if they know the correct magic word, choose not to use it and their parents don't seem to notice or mind or are not quite sure how to correct it.

From the start

As soon as your toddler starts learning to talk, start teaching them to say, "Please," and "Thank you."

Prompt them to say, "Please," as soon as you realise they want something, which they may indicate by pointing and after they have been given it, prompt and cajole them into saying, "Thank you." Of course, when they actually start asking it's easier to encourage these valuable words out of them and praise them each time they attempt to use them, especially if they were unprompted. But there is no point getting angry or frustrated when they forget. They are not going to learn it immediately or always remember to say it, but it is important you say it every time to them. Again, if they are asked if they would like something, the answer is either, "Yes, please," or "No, thank you," where appropriate.

School-age children
If school-age children forget to say, "Please," firstly prompt them but if they continue not to say it, explain that neglecting to ask correctly means they will simply not get what they asked for. Wait and if necessary, prompt a, "Thank you." But never say it for them, too many parents say the 'thank you' in a slightly sarcastic tone when it is not forthcoming. Children must say the words themselves. If they defiantly choose not to say, "Thank you," when possible take back whatever it was they have just been given, which will get their attention immediately.

Teenagers
Even teenagers who certainly do know better can still forget the all important "Please"' and "Thank you," or sometimes they are lost as they trail off sentences. Teenagers are still our children and although we don't want to embarrass them (or ourselves) in front of their friends by asking, "What's the magic word?" and lose any street cred we may have had, we can still have a quiet reminder with them.

By example
Make sure you are always polite whether it is to your children, trades people or sales persons and remember to thank other car drivers if they show courtesy towards you. It infuriates me when I let someone out onto a busy road (when I can see they've been waiting a long time) and they don't even bother to say, "Thank you."

Thank you letters
In this era of mobile phones, e-mails and text messaging, the art of a written thank you letter seems almost Dickensian and as long as one says thank you,

does it much matter how it's done?

But to the recipient of the thank you message, it does. Very little time or effort goes into a 'thanx nan 4 the £10, lv Billy'. But a short hand written note or card shows effort and thought, even though the thought (if we're honest) has probably been at a parent's insistence. Grandparents, godparents, aunts, family friends often keep these letters or cards and even display them and show them to their friends. It's not just parents who are proud of polite children.

The younger the child, the shorter the note will be, to the point of you writing the thank you bit and your child just signing it. But as they get older encourage them to say what they want to say even if you write it down first and they copy it, but let it be in their own words. This may take a little prompting, for example, 'Dear Nana, thank you for the £10. Love Billy', is a bit short, so get them to say what they are going to do with the money and always get them to ask how the person they are writing to is. 'How are you Nana? I hope you are well. I hope we get to see you soon.' Prompting children to enquire about someone's well-being, whether in a letter or by asking, teaches them to take an interest in other people.

By the time children are teenagers if they stay over at a friend's house or are taken out to supper by a friend's parents they should write a letter of thanks.

Try and encourage your child occasionally to write cards and letters to their grand-parents to let them know what they've been up to and ask how they are. Everyone enjoys receiving letters and your children will be just as enthusiastic when they receive a reply to theirs. Wouldn't it be sad if when your children are adults they had no love letters to look back on. Texting and e-mailing is brilliant but it will never replace the art of the written letter.

We are all very quick to complain if we have had bad service but how often do we thank people for good service? For instance, if you have a child entertainer come to your child's birthday party and everyone enjoyed him, help your child to write a short note of thanks to him. And encourage this practice as they grow up.

Excuse-me

Although we are regularly encouraging our children's verbal skills and teaching them to interact with adults they also have to learn the polite way to interrupt other people's conversation.

Children need to be taught that if they wish to interrupt someone to say something they must wait for a pause, then say, "Excuse-me, please." They will probably need your help with learning exactly how to do this the first few times. Again, when children manage this unprompted for the first few times, acknowledge it either by praise or by catching their eye and nodding your approval and smile.

If a child needs to attract an adult's attention they should also use "Excuse-me,". For example, "Excuse-me please, do you know where Mr Ree, the English teacher is?"

"Excuse-me," is also used as an apology. For instance, children must learn to say, "Excuse-me," if they need to pass close by to someone in a congested space such as on public transport or in a supermarket as a way of saying, "Sorry, but I'm going to have to squeeze by you." They should also learn to use it by way of apology if they sneeze, cough, burp or pass wind (noisily!) in the close proximity of another person.

Coughing and sneezing

Only by telling and showing children what to do will they know. So when the situation arises explain to children how to cover their mouth if they are coughing and how to cover their mouth and nose if they are sneezing, preferably into a tissue and then say, "Excuse-me."

Nobody wants to sit at a table eating only to have someone, child or adult, sneeze all over them and the food, it's unhygenic and extremely unpleasant.

As they get older explain that if they are sitting at a table eating how they must turn their heads away from the table and the person next to them if they feel a cough or sneeze coming. However, if they have diners on each side they will have to try and push back their chair to cough and sneeze (out of the line of fire) then say, "Excuse-me."

Yawning

Encourage children to put a hand over their mouths when they yawn. They must also avoid yawning when being spoken to, either individually or in a group.

'Pardon?' not 'Wot?'

Very self-explanatory, teach your children to say, "Pardon?" or "Sorry?" not,

"What?" or "Wot?" It just sounds so much more polite. Each time they say, "What?" or "Wot?" ask them to say, "Pardon?" or "Sorry?" even if they don't consider them part of the new Yoof culture. Consistency is the name of the game here. Your children will be no different to anyone else's if you start from day one and are still reminding them when they're fourteen! Have no fear eventually it will sink in.

Shaking hands

'You never get a second chance to make a first impression,' so the saying goes and rightly or wrongly many of us judge a person's character by their handshake. To me and to many people the limp handshake and the averted eyes scream this person is wet, lacking in personality and ineffectual. But eye to eye contact and a firm handshake says open, honest, confident and capable. This is not to say we are always right but it is our first impression and we should teach our children to make a good first impression. It could eventually mean the difference between them getting the job they wanted or not.

From about the age of ten, boys and girls should be taught how to shake hands correctly. Even from this age there will be many occasions when they will use it. Children should be taught to look the person in the eye and give a firm handshake, the emphasis being on firm, not bone-crushing or limp. Explain that if they think their hands are a bit clammy to try and dry them first without being noticed. However, if they shake hands with someone who has clammy hands to avoid immediately wiping their hands down their trousers or skirt, although this is everyone's instant reaction. As they shake hands, they look the person in they eye and say, "How do you do?" Or introduce themselves.

Opening doors and ladies first

Your own opinions on feminism and women's lib may determine whether you think boys should still be brought up to show women traditional courtesies, but in my opinion women today, and I'm sure in the future, will still very much appreciate them.

Boys can start being taught how and why they should open doors and car doors for women from about the age of seven. Opportunities will often arise for them to practice. A quiet prompt to your son suggesting he opens the car door for his Nana, and after his Nana is safely in her seat, to shut it, not just to leave it for her to shut. This polite gesture will without doubt be met with a few kind words and a smile which is encouragement in itself for any child to do it again at the next opportunity.

When you are out shopping if you see someone struggling at a shop door with a pushchair or see an elderly person simply struggling with the weight of it, point it out to your child then ask your son (or daughter in these circumstances) to open it for them. You will be surprised how well small gestures like these are received by strangers and your child will again be encouraged to repeat it at another time. In addition to the thanks and praise he or she will receive from the grateful recipients, praise the child yourself.

Teach your son (when appropriate) to open doors for women and to let them walk through first. Also explain that if he and a member of the opposite sex both went to do something at the same time, i.e. enter a doorway or join a queue, to allow the female to go first.

Helping with coats

As soon as boys are tall enough actually to be of assistance with helping

"Nana, you've got a new hairstyle."

someone on with their coat, start to encourage it. And by helping on with a coat I mean holding the coat open so the person can easily slip their arms in, not just passing them their coat and letting them sort it out for themselves (yes, I've known a few of those guys too). Firstly let your son help you and then your female friends and relatives. The attention your son will get from the ladies will again spur him onto help again until it becomes second nature.

How to pay a compliment

Now you may not think that we should have to teach boys how to pay a compliment and that it should come naturally. But isn't one of women's greatest complaints against men that they never pay us enough compliments, if any? So let's tackle the problem at the core and teach them. Girls never seem to have the same problem and they are usually very open with compliments.

Fortunately teaching boys how to pay a compliment also teaches them to be observant which will be an invaluable lesson for all areas of their life.

We all enjoy feeling flattered when we are paid a compliment whether it be from a fourteen year-old boy or a seventy year-old man. And again the reaction (positive attention) boys receive from the opposite sex after they have paid a compliment will encourage them to continue.

Men equally enjoy being paid a compliment. So say how great you think your teenager son's new haircut is, or tell your partner how sharp he looks in his new linen suit.

The easiest way to start teaching your son how to make a compliment is from his father or a father figure. Single mums and dads will have to teach children themselves. Explain to your partner that prior to you being almost ready for a night out, he must tell his son that when Mummy enters the room, he should tell her how pretty she looks or how much he likes her dress, because it would make her very happy. When you are ready and dressed to kill, long dress, hair up, nails painted, teetering on your Manolos, *you wish*, walk elegantly into the room where your son and partner are. Your partner should say something first as an example and he may have to prompt his son. But as soon as your son says something complimentary, look surprised, delighted, thank him and make a fuss of him. If you are a single parent, when your son sees you dressed up, ask him if he thinks Mummy looks pretty, he will undoubtedly say yes, then explain that if ever he thinks Mummy is looking special to say how pretty she looks, or if he particularly likes her dress to say so, because it would make her very happy. Make a fuss of him.

If you know your mother is coming to see you but she is visiting the hairdresser first, tell your son and suggest, if he thinks it looks good, to tell her how nice her hair looks when she visits. Grandmother's reaction will be proof enough that compliments work.

Obviously at first we are teaching children what to say, regardless of what they think, which screams of insincerity, but what it teaches them is to be more observant about other people's appearance and how a simple compliment can really make someone's day. If I've just been to the hairdressers and someone says my hair looks great, even if they don't really think so, frankly, I don't give a damn, because it makes me feel good.

When young boys first realise that a few kind words to the ladies brings about a smile and that flattered, 'do you really think so' look, they use it rather indiscriminately. Teachers, family friends even sisters can suddenly all be on the receiving end of a bit of flattery but don't worry boys do settle down and become selective.

Girls can also be taught to pay compliments although it does seem so much more natural to them. But there is no reason why girls cannot be taught to compliment the opposite sex when they look good. Starting with their dads.

Apologies

It goes without saying that there will be times when your children are going to have to apologise for their actions, so they must learn how to say they are sorry in a way that the recipient actually believes they are.

With toddlers, the most common misdemeanours are snatching toys from a friend and hitting. As with all incidents, make sure you know exactly what happened, i.e. was your child hit first and hit back. It doesn't make things any better but at least you must make both children apologise and the one who 'started' the altercation, apologise first.

Sometimes with toddlers you'll find yourself apologising on their behalf as they simply cannot cope with their feelings of anger or humiliation. They don't think they've done anything wrong.

Teach children how to say they are sorry. They must try and look the person in the eye and say, 'I'm sorry.' Some children find apologising much harder than others, but never let them get away with turning away and spitting out a, 'SORRY.' Calmly insist they say it again correctly. If you raise your voice as in, 'SAY YOU ARE SORRY,' they are far more likely to come out with an equally loud, 'SORRY'. You may even have to cajole it out of them, 'Come on darling, say you are sorry and then we can get on and do something far more fun.'

Your children are at full-time school and they tell you about an incident that happened in their class. For example, they were chatting and messing around in a lesson and the teacher gave them a conduct mark or detention. Tell them to go and see the teacher on a one-to-one basis and apologise for acting in that way and disrupting the class. They will probably still have the punishment, but the apology will be very gratefully received and the teacher will feel that the child actually was sorry, and they may well be more lenient if it happened again.

The word 'sorry' can mend a lot of bridges and placate a lot of hurt feelings.

'I want' never gets

"I want...I want!" is a demand that should strictly be the preserve of adults, as in, "I want a Ferrari, I want a villa in the South of France." And when you start funding your own lifestyle you can shout, stamp your feet and scream, "I want..I want..I want," as much as you like.

Children, however, are dependent on other people for things, mostly their parents, so they must learn to ask correctly.

Teach them always to say, "Please may I have..?" And every time they start a sentence with "I want..." calmly correct them and insist that they ask correctly. Then praise them, even if their request is turned down.

Obviously, it's very easy for them to start with "I want.." as it often follows the question, "Do you want.." or "What do you want?" So try to avoid the 'wants' and use "Would you like.."
The response being, "I would like..."

Don't get angry when they forget, just simply keep reminding them. It will not happen overnight, but gradually it will sink in, and when the day arrives when your little darling asks unprompted to someone outside the family, "Please may I have..?" you will beam with pride.

Reliability

A very important lesson for children to learn (and some adults I can think of!) is reliability. If you say you are going to do something, you do it. Your children will learn this lesson by your approach to reliability and pointing out the consequences to them.

For instance, if my daughter said she needed some green tissue paper for a school project the following day and I said I would get it and didn't, I have let her down. The knock on effect is she will not have the paper for the project and she will feel let down. I said I would deliver and I didn't. The other knock on effect is that my daughter may have been working with a group who have also been let down, but to them it is my daughter who was unreliable.

Children must realise how important it is that they can be counted on, relied on to do what they have said they will do and a very early way of experiencing this is at school when they are a member of a team.

As an example, if our children are in a sports team and they have a match on a Saturday morning, but Saturday morning arrives and it's freezing cold, there's a howling wind and it's raining, they may well take one look at the weather, and think they'd rather stay in bed. We take one look at the weather and think we would definitely rather stay in bed. Our children say they don't want to go or they may even feign illness and ask us to call in sick on their behalf.

Now we have the choice of staying in a warm bed or standing in the freezing cold for over an hour cheering them on. As we are human, it will take less than a nano second to know which most of us would prefer to do, but sadly that is not what we should do. By allowing our children to stay in, even trying to justify our action by thinking, well, perhaps they are unwell and at least the reserve will get to play, we are teaching them that it is OK to let people down when it suits them.

We may well have to cajole them out of bed with a few of these points, but in an encouraging not nagging tone:-
"That you are part of a team and the other members will expect you to turn up and play."
"You were delighted to be picked for the team."
"If everyone thought they could miss today, there wouldn't even be a team."
"That other people are depending on you and you simply cannot let them down."
"Please do not expect me to fib on your behalf."
"You were picked for the team because you are good, so get out there and show them exactly how good."
"Actually I would also like to stay in bed this morning but we both know what's right and I'll take a flask of hot chocolate and some biscuits."

Take another example. Around the home, if you ask your children to do something and they agree, such as tidying up the sitting room before your friends arrive at 4 o'clock for tea. By 3.45 if it is still not done, tell them in a calm but authoritative voice, "You won't let me down now, will you? You told me you would do it and I am relying on you."

If they fail to do it, there is no point shouting and screaming at them, it is far more effective to tell them how very disappointed you are in them, and how badly they have let you down. Explain the importance of being a dependable person, not just around the home, but at school and especially in the workplace. However, do not let your children off the hook, insist they still tidy up after your friends have gone and they can wash up the tea things as well, as a reminder to do things when asked.

Children who are not taught how to be reliable will grow up and constantly let friends and co-workers down. Even as teenagers their friends will soon get fed up with them if they continually say they will go with them somewhere and then at the last minute decide not to. Of course, everyone has a right to a change of mind, but all involved parties must agree.

The more reliable you are as a parent, the more natural it will be for your children to become reliable, so think very carefully before promising to do something for them that you can't actually carry through.

Point out to your children the importance of being on time, whether it is for lessons, social dates or appointments. Explain how discourteous it is to be late but if they are, always to make sure they apologise.

HOW TO BEHAVE AT SCHOOL

Introduction to nursery school

Toddlers strive for independence and nursery school offers them their first real step towards becoming independent. A good nursery education can be a very valuable and important part of your child's development, not to mention the benefit of a few hours break for you.

The nursery will provide a wonderful opportunity for your children to interact with other children and to accept authority from other adults. The teachers should promote and encourage good manners and respect in your children through good practice and example. However, it will be the parents' continual effort in teaching social skills and discipline at home that will benefit their child the most.

For many children, it will be their first opportunity to learn to interact with other children, to learn to share and to have to wait their turn. It will probably be the first time children choose who they wish to become friends with rather than playing with some children of their parents' friends. Having to make choices, coping without their parents and learning self-control are all valuable lessons for your children. They will also enjoy the stimulation from new activities.

Preparing your children for nursery

During the weeks leading up to the start of nursery, talk to your children about it in very favourable and positive ways. If you are finger painting or making something with your child explain how many more new activities they will be able to try and how many little friends they will make and how they will be able to invite them around for tea. Encourage them to ask questions about it. Find out the nursery's agenda for the morning and then explain exactly what will happen so that there are no surprises that may cause anxiety. Reassure them that after you have introduced them to their teachers and they join the other children, you will leave. Explain that during the morning they will play, paint, have a drink and a snack, play outdoors, be read a story and then you will be back to pick them up.

But do make sure for the first few weeks that you are on time so that when the door opens the first thing they see will be you waiting.

First day

Decide together what they will wear the day before they start; even at this age they can have very set ideas about clothing, especially girls. The last thing you want is a confrontation on the first morning, where your daughter is insisting on wearing her satin cream party dress without knickers. It is best to put out two suitable outfits and let her choose. However, if she insists on the satin cream party dress, let her wear it and secretly put a set of more suitable clothes in the car, in case when she sees the rest of the class in more casual clothes she may wish to change. After all, we're all guilty of overdressing for some do or another.

Even the most confident children can feel suddenly nervous when it is time for a parent to leave so if your child cries when you are about to go, don't worry, children settle down very quickly once their parents have gone. Parents can often be as anxious at having to leave as children are about having to stay, but don't let this reflect in your face. Give your child a big smile and leave. Then if you just can't help it, go and have a good blub.

When you go to pick them up from nursery, make sure they say, "Thank you," and "Goodbye," to their teacher. On your way home ask your children what they did and if they met anyone they liked. Praise them for being so grown-up in going to nursery and how proud you are of them.

There will be many occasions when you are brought back the latest painting or cardboard and tissue masterpiece. Apart from saying how lovely they are, when you get home, sit down with your child and actually ask them about their pieces of work; "Where did they get the idea from?" "Why did they choose those particular colours?" "Where exactly are the ears?"

Any interaction is always encouraging speech. They will have to think about their answers, and they will be very flattered that you have taken such an interest in something which they have probably spent all morning on, and will give them confidence for their next little project. Of course, if you can find a fridge door, or a wall to hang it on, all the better.

Preparing for school

To prepare your children for full-time schooling, it is far more important that they have conquered the basic social skills rather than cracked trigonometry and Russian for beginners.

School is an institution for education and learning; not a babysitting service. Teachers are there to teach, and with your help and support, your child will be able to get the most out of the system.

Every parent hopes that their children will do well at school, and preparing them so that they are socially equipped to cope with their new surroundings is their responsibility.

The move from nursery school to primary school can be very daunting for children. They may feel overwhelmed by the sheer size of the building, the larger classrooms, and the numbers, size and age of the older children.

So it is up to you to make their transition and future life at school as enjoyable and trouble-free as possible. They should be socially equipped and confident to take on the new challenges they are about to face and in doing so they will need to be taught the following:-

* Discipline (as in understanding and obeying simple instructions)
* What to expect at school
* Respecting adults
* Listening skills
* Respecting their peers
* How to take turns
* How to dress and undress
* Table manners
* Getting involved
* Toilet training
* Homework

Parent/teacher support

Throughout your child's education, your support, not only of your child but also of their teachers, will be vital.

A teacher should always be informed if anything has happened at home that may affect your child's behaviour or attitude at school. Parental situations are usually one of the main causes; arguments, separations, issues with step-parents or parent's partners, past and present, can all become the focus of distress in a child. So rather than wait for the teacher to contact you, if circumstances change at home, a short note or quiet word with the teacher will alert them to the possibility of future problems. A teacher who knows a child's parents have just divorced is likely to be far more sympathetic to a no-show of homework than one who doesn't.

If your child is finding a particular subject difficult, try to see their teacher. Failing that, fax or e-mail them asking what you can do to positively help. Giving that extra support and encouragement at home will not only be helping your child reach the class standard but will make their teacher's job easier.

Make sure that when your child starts school they have everything that the school has requested, whether it is uniform, sports clothes, art overalls, pens or pencils. A child can perceive any shortfall as inadequacy.

Teachers will occasionally have special requests, such as collecting cardboard or plastic boxes etc, perhaps for an art or science project, so make the effort to contribute. When extra help is needed for the school fete, offer your help; it is far too easy to sit back and think someone else will do it. It is also setting an excellent example for your child to see you giving up your time.

Discipline

Teachers are employed to teach subjects to your children, not social graces and basic discipline.

By the time they attend primary school, children should respect the authority of adults and act accordingly upon their requests or orders. They should have been taught to respect other people's property, so that they do not draw on walls or desks or damage property etc. If they wish to speak to the teacher, they put their hand up and wait to be addressed; they do not simply shout out. Common courtesies such as, "Please," "Thank you," and "Excuse me," should by now, be second nature to them.

What to expect

Talk to your child over a period of time, telling them what to expect when they arrive at school. (Probably best to skip over the awful food and smelly changing rooms.) Ask if they are worried or scared about any aspect of their new challenge, and try to dispel their anxieties. Find out the general timetable of the day so that you can explain to your child what will be happening throughout the day. Is there an assembly, how long are the playground breaks, do they eat with the rest of the school or do the juniors eat first? Is your child having a packed or school lunch? If they are going to have a packed lunch, what would they like?

Respecting adults

By the time your children go to school they should already respect adults, but they may think that it only applies to their teachers. Explain to them that the lunch supervisors, class assistants, school secretaries and cleaning staff should all be treated with the same respect as the teachers. Children can sometimes behave differently to those they perceive as not having much authority.

Even from a young age, they must start to learn to obey authority. Children who already respect adults are the ones who are going to sit down and listen to their teacher unlike the children who have never learnt to respect anybody or anything, who are going to be disruptive in the class and scratch their names on their desks.

Apart from the obvious use of "Please," and "Thank you," there are many more opportunities that children can apply them during their normal school day.
For instance getting off the school bus and turning to the driver with a, "Thank you, bye," would probably be appreciated and noticed amongst the dozens who say nothing.

Children should be reminded to always make the effort to thank a teacher who has organised something whether it was a trip, a show or an art exhibition. Teachers put a great deal of their own time and effort into projects at school and a thank you from a grateful pupil and parent goes a long way to making their effort worthwhile.

Remind your children to smile and say, "Please," and "Thank you," to the lunch supervisors and if they happen to pass the secretaries or cleaning staff in the corridors, a smile and a "Hello," or "Good morning," will usually prompt, after the initial shock, a pleasant response.

Never underestimate the value adults put on polite children.

Encourage them to be observant and courteous, explain for instance that if they see a teacher, or even another pupil, anywhere in the school, struggling with an armful of books and trying to open a door that they should open it for them or offer to help.

It is well worth explaining some situations like these may arise at school and how best they can help. Let's face it, it's not rocket science that children who are courteous and well-behaved at school have a much easier school life than those who are not.

Don't worry if you think you are about to turn your child into the class creep, you are not, you are simply teaching your child to be courteous and aware of others; a lesson they will take into life that will always be appreciated.

Listening skills

To listen to others without interrupting is an imperative quality for any aged schoolchild, and a few adults we all know!

Their pre-school listening education comes from you reading to them, talking to them, encouraging them to ask questions and then listening to your answers and vice versa. Listening is give and take. You listen and then you can respond to what has been said. (Building listening skills, page 61)
A child who is constantly interrupting the teacher, by either talking out of turn or talking to another child, disrupts the entire class. Don't let it be yours.

Respecting their peers

Children need other children, they need friends, or otherwise school will be a very solitary, unkind world. And, not unlike ourselves, your children will make friends at school, some of whom may remain friends for life, so they need to know how to treat them.

Young children very often have different 'best friends' every week. If, however, they seem upset about a friendship, ask them to explain to you what happened and offer advice on how to resolve the problem.

Encourage your child to try and be friendly with everyone, although obviously there will be some children they prefer to others, and discourage them from joining in with name calling or isolating certain children. Explain how awful they would feel if it was them being called names or not included in playground games.

Tell them that if they see a child upset in the absence of a teacher, to go and ask what the problem is, or to go and find a teacher to help them.

How to take turns

Unfortunately, many children have no idea how to wait for their turn, which will immediately create a disturbance in the class. A good way to teach children how to wait patiently is by playing plenty of board games at home, and the more people playing, the longer they have to wait their turn.

Learning to wait your turn is not the only advantage to playing board or card games. The time spent with the family is very definitely positive time; the children will be in seventh heaven because they have your undivided attention, it encourages speech, hopefully fun and laughter, a certain amount of thought and strategy (depending on the game) and proof that life exists beyond television.

How to dress and undress

By the time children go to school full-time, they should be able to dress and undress themselves, as they will have to do this for PE. So, however much you have enjoyed dressing and undressing your little darlings, you have done them a disservice if they are incapable of doing it themselves by the time they reach school age.

One of teachers' perennial complaints is the number of children who just stand in the cloakroom and expect an adult to undress and dress them. They do not even seem to have a clue about putting on shoes and socks. Imagine if every child was like that, the PE lesson would be over before all the class were even changed. Even more amazing when you consider that they could all probably programme a video recorder!

Let your child practice getting in and out of their school uniform before the start

of term. They will also feel less conspicuous in it if they have already worn it a few times around their home. Children should also be told that when they take off their clothes to fold them or hang them up and not just drop them on a heap on the changing room floor *(I know, I know)*. Sewing large loops into their school uniforms will make this task much easier for them. (Although it probably won't make the slightest bit of difference!)

Obviously, children mature and develop at different times, and where one child may easily be able to tie laces and deal with buttons, some may take a little longer. Be patient and keep practising and giving encouragement. Comments such as, 'You'll be the only one in your class who will need help dressing,' will cause unnecessary anxiety and undermine their confidence. Be kind, supportive and positive. If your child has not mastered laces and buttons, buy shoes with velcro and let your child's teacher know that they have not yet perfected doing up buttons but are trying hard, and in the meantime will wear a sweatshirt or sweater.

Teaching-aid soft toys dressed in clothes with buttons, zips and laces to help children learn these skills.

Table manners

Hopefully, if you have been teaching table manners to your children (see table manner page 69, they are now very capable of using, or trying to use, a knife, fork and spoon correctly. They will, however, be shocked and amused about the eating habits of some of their school friends and be very quick to regale you with stories about them.

You could point out that if they see one of their friends struggling with their knife and fork, they should offer to show them how to use them with a quiet comment such as, 'My Mum says it easier if you try like this…'. Explain to your child the importance of never embarrassing or humiliating their friends. Children who are struggling while their friends are not will automatically feel slightly embarrassed, which can manifest itself in a show of bravado by eating in a more ridiculous way to raise a laugh.

It's very normal to find their table manners deteriorate once they have school lunches, but a few simple reminders at dinner will soon put them back on the right track.

Getting involved

Find out at the beginning of each term what extra activities will be on offer, and then encourage your children to join in. School plays, shows, competitions, sport, clubs, whatever it is, suggest they give it a try.

If, for instance, there is an audition for a school production, encourage them to go along and try out for it. If they don't get offered a part or they don't like the idea of being on stage, tell them to ask about helping behind the scenes, with lighting, costumes, scenery or programmes. It is so important for kids to get involved with projects. It teaches them to get on with other pupils, often of different ages, and to work with their teachers in an 'out of classroom' environment. Working with a team towards a common goal, taking responsibilities they may otherwise not have, taking or even giving orders and making suggestions is a worthwhile, confidence building experience. The pride and excitement they will feel 'on the night' will spur them on to contribute again.

Not unlike life, the more they put into it, the more they will get out of it.

Toilet trained

Explain to your child if they need to go the toilet during a lesson, they will have to raise their hand, wait to be spoken to by the teacher, then ask, "Please may I be excused?" Make sure that your child can get in and out of their clothes easily when they get there and as basic as it may seem, do make sure they can use toilet paper properly. If not, they could end up in a very embarrassing situation which could result in teasing from their classmates. Finally, remind them not to leave bits of toilet paper or tissues on the floor of the toilet cubicle and to always wash their hands before returning to the classroom. Remind little boys to put the toilet seat up to have a wee and then put it down again and to wash their hands.

Homework

Why children under the age of 12 are given homework beats me. Reading I can understand but they work all day at school and then they have up to one hour's homework that can take twice as long. When are they meant to have time to just be children?

Anyway, the best approach to homework is to let your children have a snack as soon as they get back from school and then get straight on and do it. If you are at home sit them down and help organise. Try and stay in the same room, whether you're preparing supper or reading the paper. Don't have a TV on. The TV is the carrot on a stick to get the work done. If your children get stuck on a question, don't just tell them the answer, show them how to work it out.

Approach other parents about their thoughts on the idea of a homework club at school, then talk to the head of the school about the possibility. If it is not feasible, discuss the chances of reducing the homework load.

WORKING PARENTS

Life is about compromise, choice and determination, and everyone has a different agenda as to why they want or have to work. The days of full-time mothers being made to feel guilty that they don't have a career or working parents feeling guilty because they are not at home (aren't) but should be well behind us.

But parents who work invariably do feel varying degrees of guilt. Unfortunately, the more guilt parents feel, the more some try to compensate for it by over indulging their children, giving them too many presents in the form of toys, gadgets, designer clothing, sweets etc and not enough attention and discipline.

"Mummy's home"

Parents who both work full-time are less likely to discipline their child for several reasons,
a) they feel they see so little of their child that when they do they don't want to start acting the disciplinarian,
b) they feel guilty about working and not being with their child, and
c) they feel too tired for any confrontations, so give in more often than not (and then feel guilty for doing so).

Children miss out on all counts. They seldom have parents at home to look after them and when they are at home their parents do not exercise proper parental control, which leads to children growing up expecting to get everything they want, a lack of discipline and a lack of respect for their parents. But it needn't be like that.

How to be a good working parent

If you do work, the best way to alleviate your guilt is by being a good parent when you are with your child. Sitting down to dinner around a table together, talking, listening, encouraging table manners, interacting, having a game and adhering to bed-time hours. The age of your children will dictate what you can do with them in the evenings.

As a working parent, you will have to take several things into consideration:-
a) You are going to be tired at the end of the day when you get home.
b) Your children will want your attention.
c) Your partner will need some attention.
d) Some type of meal will have to be organised.

Only one parent home in time for supper

If only one parent can be home in time for supper with the young children, sit with them while they eat, but wait until your partner comes home to eat with him/her.

Children should help to lay the table and be encouraged to help with preparing supper, however simple. The parent, or single parents, should sit at the table with their children while they eat, talk to them and in an unobtrusive, positive way, correct their table manners. When they have finished, let them help clear the plates and wash up or load the dishwasher. This is also a good time to chat and laugh with them. If there is time before the bedtime routine starts, play a game, do some drawing or just sit and have a chat and a cuddle together.

If everyone is fairly tired, sometimes parents can just cuddle their children in front of a short video or TV programme which can be discussed on the way to bed. However, try and not let this become a habit as regularly sitting in front of the TV will be of very little benefit to anyone.

Both parents

If both parents are home early enough the family can all eat together and should take it in turns to do the bedtime routine. It is very tempting for parents who have been out all day to let their children stay up later, but do stick to the bedtime routine. If a bath is part of the bedtime routine a child can really benefit from the one-to-one time with a parent sharing their bath (depending on the child's age). Then, once children are asleep parents can have some of that all-important adult time with each other.

Children love to have something to look forward to, so parents should plan, in advance something fun to do together at the weekend with their children and talk to them about it during the week. It should be centred around an activity which does not include buying something for them. Parents' time is far more important than the instant gratification of a present. What parents decide to do will depend on their children's ages and the weather, so it could be anything from building a camp in their bedroom to a picnic.
As the weekend approaches children will have something to really look forward to with their parents, so it is terribly important that they are not let down.

Parents will sleep better and feel less guilt (thus be less stressed) when they realise that the time they do spend with their children is beneficial quality time.

Weekend fathers
With both parents working full-time, the father can find it difficult to define his role as a parent, because mothers tend to take over in the evening and at the weekends. But fathers can still spend invaluable time with their children. Weekends are the perfect time for fathers to take their children on one-to-one outings which are so important for them and a bonding time for both. If there is more than one child, the mother should take the other child for a different outing and then the family can meet up later in the day. If fathers are home during the week, in time for their children's bedtime routine, they should take turns with the children's mother in carrying it out. And don't be surprised or hurt if young children suddenly insist on having one parent in favour of another. It literally is just a phase.

CHILD CARE
HOW YOU CAN STILL BE IN CONTROL

At some point during bringing up your children you will probably need some type of child-care. Exactly what type you choose will depend on many things:

- Do you require someone to just help you around the house and occasionally babysit?
- Will you be working part-time or full-time and need someone who can take sole charge of a pre-schooler in your absence?
- Do you want someone to take sole charge of your baby or toddler a couple of afternoons a week so you can simply have a break?
- Will you employ someone to come to your home or use a day-care centre? In which case you will have little control.
- Do you just need someone to help at home and pick the children up from school and babysit until you get home?
- Do you want someone to live-in?
- How much can you afford?

Which child-care route you choose to take will dictate just how much influence you have, if any, over the care of your child in your absence. To be honest choosing the right person can be a bit of a lottery, but it is of the utmost importance that you employ someone who you really feel you can trust with your baby or child's welfare. Always, always follow up references to check they are bona fide.

Employing someone at home

Continuity
Unfortunately, the days when the nannies used to stay until charges had left home are a thing of the past. This is one of the nightmares of child-care these days - duration. How long will your help stay; three months, six months, a year, two if you are very lucky, so it is very important that all these different girls are taught how to bring up your child in exactly the same way, so that your child's upbringing has some continuity.

"Yes please. Thanks!"

Teaching your nanny how to bring up your children

Regardless of what type of help you have employed and for the sake of this chapter I'm going to call them all nannies. Even if you are out to work you must still be in control of your child's upbringing. After all, how can you expect anyone to know how you want your children brought up? How can a nanny teach your child table manners when they may not eat correctly themselves? Even if you just have your children cared for after school, make sure that your discipline and standards are continued by whoever is babysitting.

I once employed a girl from Croatia and after taking the children to school I came back to find her eating four fried eggs straight from the frying pan with a tablespoon! I found myself not only teaching my own children table manners but the help as well.

Never feel intimidated or embarrassed by explaining very carefully exactly how you want a nanny to care for your child. Leave yourself plenty of time on their first day to explain. Ask her if there is anything she does not understand about your instructions, as she may be too embarrassed to ask. If you leave it a week or so to start explaining, it will appear as though you are not happy with the way she has been doing things. Establish this at the very beginning and write it down, along with contact telephone numbers for you and your partner, your doctor, friends, relatives and neighbours, in fact anyone who could help in an emergency and leave the numbers of the emergency services. Different countries have different emergency numbers.

Explain the following to your nanny:

Toddlers and young children

Tantrums

Explain exactly how you want your nanny to deal with tantrums, otherwise it is far too easy for your sitter to simply give in to their demands. After all, she will not be around in the future to see the results of her lack of control.

Discipline

Explain to your nanny what she must do if the children misbehave. She must never smack or hit your children or shake babies or toddlers to try to get them to stop crying.

Meals and snacks

What they will have for their meals, what they are allowed to drink and if any sweets, snacks or biscuits are allowed.

To sit with them while they eat, and depending on what stage they are with implements, how they should hold them and how you like them to behave at the table. All too often children are given their tea or supper and left to get on with it, while the nanny reads a magazine and has a cup of tea in another part of the kitchen. The children must wait until they ask or wait until she tells them that they can get down from the table. The children should help clear their plates.

Naps

Exactly what time your children have their nap(s), for how long and how to wake them if they oversleep. There is a tendency for some nannies, who don't live-in, to let babies and toddlers sleep as much as they want during the day, as it makes their life so much easier (and they're not the ones who are going to be up all night with a wide awake child).

NB If you have help looking after your baby, depending on which school of baby-care you adhere to, how long you want them to leave your toddler crying before they attend to him or her.

Things to do with your child

Explain to your nanny what games your child likes to play and how to play them, i.e. hide and seek, a simple board game, Lego. Suggest an activity that they must do with the child, perhaps painting or making something and show them where everything necessary for the activity can be found.

If you would like them to have some fresh air and exercise or if they go to the park to take something to play with, such as a ball or tricycle, and what to take as a snack. Explain the importance of sun cream protection.

Ask your nanny to encourage your child to help with making the beds or dusting and to help clear up their toys and room.

Ask them to enrol the help of your child to lay the table for you and your partner, so that when you return you can feign surprise and praise and thank them for being so kind. This type of response and attention will encourage them to be helpful again.

Encouraging good behaviour

Ask your nanny to prompt your children to say, "Please," and "Thank you." Ask her to praise and encourage them when they are helpful, polite or being creative. If they take them on public transport or to public places explain how you would like them to behave.

TV, videos, DVDs and computer games

There is a big temptation for the nanny to have the TV on the entire day, which is not what you want as it is too easy for your child to watch it all day. Explain which programmes, if any, or videos your child can watch and for how long. You must set a time limit. No TV while they are eating.

Accidents

Not to get angry and humiliate your child if he/she wets their pants or accidentally knocks over something in the home.

Safety in the home

In the kitchen she must keep children away from all sharp knives and to turn any saucepan handles on the hob inwards. Never leave an iron on, or cooling, where it can be pulled down. Never leave a bath running, a full bath or a child alone in the bathroom or the bath, even for a second.

Make sure she knows where your first aid kit and/or plasters are kept.

Bedtime

If you are not going to be home to put your children to bed, it is very important that your nanny knows exactly what the routine is so that she can follow it right down to the book you are reading to them.

If you are usually home for the bedtime routine but are going to be late, let her know if it is likely to be before or after your child is asleep. This way she can explain to the children that they can wait for you to arrive but they must remain in their beds, perhaps looking at a book or playing with a toy.
Explain your policy of taking them straight back to bed if they get out.

Changes in behaviour

Whatever method of child-minding you choose watch for any changes in your children's behaviour that may indicate that they are not happy. Children in child-care centres, and to an extent nurseries, have to vie for adult attention with other children. Some children who may seem perfectly confident at home, may feel shy and unable to mix away from the home environment.

• Have they become withdrawn and less communicative?

• Do they become very distressed about having to go to child-care or be left with their nanny in the mornings?

• Have they become more aggressive towards you or their siblings?

• Are they seeking more attention at home by behaving badly, throwing tantrums?

If your children are experiencing any of these symptoms, don't get annoyed with them. Find out what has caused the change in behaviour. Take them somewhere quiet, sit down and give them a cuddle and tell them about your day. Then ask them about their day. Prompt them with questions, such as, "Are there any naughty children at the centre?" "What do they do there?", "Who are their friends?" "Are there any children they are not so keen on? Have any of the staff at the centre changed?" In the gentlest possible way try and coax out of them exactly what has been happening so you can try and interpret exactly what is disturbing them. Discuss their behaviour with whoever looks after them. Ask the day-centre or nursery to be extra vigilant in watching exactly what is going on with your child.

If your children are looked after at home it is a little more worrying. It may be that your children are not being looked after according to your instructions or that they are simply not getting enough parental attention. So, firstly, make a conscious effort to give them more of your time by playing, talking and reading to see if the problem resolves itself. Also, ask their nanny, in a very calm voice, if she has noticed a change in their behaviour during the day, if any issues have arisen that have become a problem between them? Does she feel she can cope? Has she had to reprimand them for anything? The possibility that she is not giving them enough attention or has slapped them must not be overlooked. However, be very diplomatic as you don't want to alienate her if she is innocent.

School-age children
It is important that your children grow to respect and help your nanny and not start talking to them as though she was a house-slave.

TV, videos, DVDs and computer games
Explain exactly how much TV they can watch and under no circumstances let them be talked into allowing 'just another 10 minutes'.

Snacks
Detail what they are allowed to have when they get home from school; it is far healthier if she makes them some wholemeal sandwiches than just gives them crisps, biscuits and sweets. Whether they can have a snack will depend on what time their supper is.

Meals
Discuss what they will have for their supper.
If they are going to eat before you get home, ask the nanny to sit with the children at the table while they eat, not in front of the TV, and encourage good table manners, making sure she knows exactly what you are expecting.
The children must ask to get down from the table or wait until they are told.
If the children are going to wait for you to eat, they can also help lay the table, as they will enjoy the extra praise they will receive.

Homework
A good routine for children to get into after school is snack, homework, play/TV time, supper, wind down and bed. If children leave the homework for too long they become too tired and uninterested to do it and by the time you return home the children will want to spend the time with you and you won't want to start helping with it.
Your nanny should help younger children organise what they have to do and sit close by in case they need help. Help should be in the form of prompting and

explaining, not simply giving them the answer. When they have finished they should put their books and pencil cases away ready for the morning, so there isn't the last minute frantic search for something.

Things to do
Once the homework is finished the children can really relax, so they may watch TV or play computer games, play with their toys; or your nanny could read them a story, depending on their ages.

Getting ready for bed
If you are going to be late home, let the nanny know if you would like the children bathed and ready for bed. Ask your nanny to engage the help of the children to hang up their clothes and pick up any toys, not to expect her to do this on her own or the children will grow up expecting it always to be done for them.

How do I know if my nanny does as I ask?
Without the use of hidden CCTV cameras and private detectives it is almost impossible to know if your nanny is following your every instruction or even some of them. You need to know that you can trust the person in charge of your children. You want to build up a mutually respectful, friendly relationship with them. Without wanting to become a spy you have every right to know what is going on in your home. With a cleaner it's very straightforward; the bathroom basin is dirty so she either failed to clean it or didn't clean it very well. You can discuss it with her next time or leave a note, it's really not that important. But someone else looking after your child is important and you are entitled to check if your wishes are being carried out, and to mention them if they are not.

Obviously it's much easier with older children as they can simply tell you what's been happening, although they are unlikely to admit to eating an entire box of cup cakes unless asked. If you suspect the children are eating too many snacks before supper ask them or your nanny. However, if we're to be totally honest we do sometimes treat nannies more leniently because we are so terrified that they may leave and plunge us into utter turmoil. But we shouldn't. They will respect us more if they know we have our finger on the pulse and that nothing slips by us (which it obviously does).

But it is much harder to know with toddlers as although toddlers can talk *and talk*, they are not always terribly reliable and are prone to exaggeration. The best way is to try and drop-in unannounced during the day once or twice in the first month. You don't have to give a reason, it's your home.

Final Word

In view of all the dire things that are happening in the world, having good manners may seem trivial. But having good manners is not really about how to eat spaghetti correctly or which fork to use. It is a consideration for other people. If we can instil in our children an empathy for others and teach them how to 'Do as you would be done by,' we are helping them to contribute to a better world. Giving up your seat in the bus, helping a mother with a pushchair through a doorway are small acts of kindness. In the larger context, such considerations have enormous ramifications. It may seem an exaggerated claim, but if we all truly thought of our fellow human beings, there could be no more bullying, vandalism, theft, abuse or exploitation. And what a great world that would be to live in.